Cambridge National

Creative iMedia

If you want to ace your Cambridge National Creative iMedia exam, there's only one thing for it — lots and lots of practice. Luckily for you, this CGP book is brimming with it.

We've included exam-style questions for Section A, plus plenty of practice for the Section B scenario-style questions too. And of course, you'll find all the answers at the back. You'll be more prepped for the exam than an A-lister on the red carpet!

Unlock your Online Edition

Just scan the QR code below or go to **cgpbooks.co.uk/extras** and enter this code!

3492 2925 6962 3611

Online Edition

By the way, this code only works for one person. If somebody else has used this book before you, they might have already claimed the code.

Exam Practice Workbook

Contents

Exam Skills 1

Section A Questions 2

Section A — Short-Answer Questions

Topic 1 — The Media Industry

Sectors 4

Products 6

Job Roles in the Media Industry 7

Topic 2 — Factors Influencing Product Design

Purpose, Language and Tone 9

Style, Content and Layout 10

Audience 11

Client Requirements 12

Client Brief Formats 13

Research Data and Methods 14

Media Codes 15

Colour, Graphics and Typography 16

Lighting, Movement and Mise-en-scène 17

Camera Techniques and Transitions 18

Audio 19

Animations and Interactivity 20

Topic 3 — Pre-Production Planning

Work Planning 21

Mind Maps and Mood Boards 22

Planning Documents 23

Storyboards and Scripts 24

Visualisation Diagrams and Wireframes 25

Protecting the Individual 26

Intellectual Property 27

Health and Safety 28

Regulation, Certification and Classification 29

Topic 4 — Distribution Considerations

Distribution Platforms 30

Distribution Media 31

File Compression 32

Image Files 33

Audio Files 34

Moving Image Files 35

Mixed Practice

Mixed Practice 36

Exam Skills 2

Section B Questions 39

Describe and Explain Questions 40

Answering 6-Mark Questions 41

Answering 9-Mark Questions 42

Section B — Scenario-Based Questions

Scenario 1 — Nostalgic Flicks 44

Scenario 2 — Rooftop Rangers 52

Scenario 3 — CPG Labs 60

Answers 68

Published by CGP

Editors: Aimee Ashurst, Sharon Keeley-Holden, Chris Lindle, Adam Worster

Author: Alex Brown
Reviewers: Mudasar Asghar and Pam Jones

With thanks to Sharon Keeley-Holden and Chris Lindle for the proofreading.
With thanks to Jade Sim for the copyright research.

Keynote presentation software is a trademark of Apple Inc., registered in the U.S. and other countries.
Microsoft PowerPoint® is a trademark of the Microsoft group of companies.

ISBN: 978 1 83774 084 0
Printed by Elanders Ltd, Newcastle upon Tyne.
Graphics from Corel® and Getty PA

Section A Questions

You'll sit a written exam that's worth **70 marks**.
It lasts **1 hour and 30 minutes** and counts for **40%** of your total grade.

The exam will start off with **Section A**, which has a total of **10 marks**.
It contains a mixture of **short-answer questions**, **multiple-choice questions** and
complete a sentence questions. Each question in Section A is worth **1 or 2 marks**.

A **command word** that is really common in Section A is **identify**.

See page 39 for information about Section B, which contains the other 60 marks.

'Identify...' questions often require you to name something

For '**identify**' questions, you usually just need to **name** something or give a **feature**.
Your answer **doesn't** need to be a full sentence.

1   Identify **one** new media **sector**.

   digital publishing ....

   [1]

Key words to pay attention to are in **bold**.

The number in the square brackets tell you how many **marks** are available.

The question tells you **how many answers** you need to give.

'**State**' questions are **similar** to 'identify' questions.

2   Identify **two** documents used to **design and plan** media products.

   1. *script* ....

   2. *wireframe layouts* ....

   [2]

'Complete...' questions ask you to fill a gap

You might be asked to fill in the **missing word or words** in a **sentence**...

3   Complete the sentence.

   The full name of Ofcom is The O*ffice* .... of C*ommunications* ....

   [2]

... or a **diagram**.

Have a go at every question — even if it's just an educated guess.

4   Complete the diagram to show the **phases** of media production.

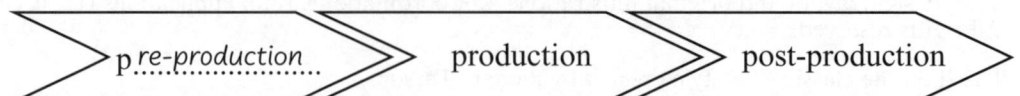

   p*re-production* > production > post-production

   [1]

Section A Questions

You might also have to complete a table

5   Complete the table with the most appropriate static image format.

Static image		
Static image format	........vector	bitmap

[2]

Mark schemes often allow multiple answers. E.g. you could name a particular file format, like JPEG for bitmaps and SVG for vectors, and still got the marks.
A bitmap is also called a 'raster' — that would be fine to write down instead of bitmap.

Multiple-choice questions ask you to tick one answer

You'll be given a choice of **four answers** and asked to **tick the box** next to the **correct** one.

6   Which of the following is **not** a category of audience segmentation?
Tick the correct box.

- ☐ age ← The answer options are ordered **alphabetically**.
- ☐ education
- ☐ interests
- ☑ purpose

It's good exam technique to use **deduction** for multiple-choice questions. This involves eliminating answers that you know can't be correct, one by one, until you only have one left.

7   Which of the following is a secondary research source?
Tick the correct box.

- ☑ books and journals
- ☐ focus groups
- ☐ interviews
- ☒ questionnaires

If you change your mind about the answer, clearly **cross out** the incorrect tick before adding another.

[1]

Top tips for answering Section A questions

1 Revise the whole course thoroughly.
There's no getting around it. These are knowledge-recall questions, so you need to have the knowledge in your brain.

This book will help you figure out what you don't know too well. Then you can go back and revise these topics.

2 Don't rush through the questions...
It's tempting to assume they are easy and race through them — read them carefully.

3 ...but, don't take too long over them either.
Remember, Section A is only worth 10 marks. Aim to spend just 10 minutes on Section A.

4 If you can, check your work before time runs out.
Once you've finished both sections A and B, you should go back and double-check your work.

Topic 1 — The Media Industry

Sectors

1 State the meaning of the term **sector**.

....

....

[1]

2 Identify the media sector that produces video for cinema releases.

....

[1]

3 Identify **one** traditional media sector other than film.

....

[1]

4 Which of the following is true for **traditional** media sectors?
Tick the correct box.

☐ They do not use computers or the internet in any way.

☐ They existed before the development of computers and the internet.

☐ They only ever deal with factual content.

☐ They were created as a result of digital technology.

[1]

5 Complete the sentence.

A newspaper is a media product produced by the print p.. sector.

[1]

6 Identify **two** ways in which the film sector has **evolved** in recent years due
to developments in technology.

1. ....

2. ....

[2]

Sectors

7 Complete the sentence.

Systems that require user input and respond to choices and actions

are produced by the i.................................... media sector.

[1]

8 Which of the following is a **new media** sector?
Tick the correct box.

☐ computer games

☐ print publishing

☐ radio

☐ television

[1]

9 Identify **two** ways content can be accessed through the **internet,** other than by using websites.

1. ....

2. ....

[2]

10 Identify the media sector which produces **eBooks**.

....

[1]

11 Identify **two** developments in digital technology which have allowed **new media** sectors to evolve.

1. ....

2. ....

[2]

Exam Tip

Some questions in the exam will ask you to complete a sentence (or sentences) with missing words. The first letter of each missing word will be given to you, so make sure you use it to help you think of a suitable word that fits the gap.

6

Products

1   Which of the following would **not** be considered a media product?
     Tick the correct box.

     ☐ multimedia

     ☐ music

     ☐ photographer

     ☐ special effects (SFX, VFX)

                                                                                    [1]

2   Identify **two** products that are used by the **digital publishing** sector.

     1. ....

     2. ....
                                                                                    [2]

3   Complete the table below to indicate if the sector uses the media product.
     One row has been completed for you.

Media sector	Tick if the media sector uses digital games	Tick if the media sector uses websites
internet	✓	✓
print publishing		
interactive media		

                                                                                    [2]

4   Identify **one** media product that is used in both the **film** and **radio** sectors.

     ....
                                                                                    [1]

5   Complete the sentence.

     AR stands for a......................... r......................... and

     VR stands for v......................... r......................... .

                                                                                    [2]

Job Roles in the Media Industry

1 Complete the table below by giving the type of job role each column of jobs falls under.

Type of role	C..................... roles	Technical roles	S..................... roles
Job	copy writer	video editor	campaign manager
	script writer	camera operator	director

[2]

2 Which **one** of the following is best described as a **creative job role**?
Tick the correct box.

☐ animator

☐ audio technician

☐ production manager

☐ web developer

[1]

3 During which production phase does a **camera operator** mainly work?

....

[1]

4 Complete the sentences.

A web d.. is responsible for the overall

look of web pages and websites across multiple platforms.

A web d.. builds websites, uploads content

and maintains working websites.

[2]

5 Identify **one** media product that is likely to be worked on by a **script writer**.

....

[1]

Exam Tip

Revise this stuff by listing the eight creative, six technical and five senior job roles under each phase of production that they are involved with. Some job roles are annoyingly easy to confuse, such as sound editor and audio technician.

Topic 1 — The Media Industry

Job Roles in the Media Industry

6 Complete the sentence.

The d............................... will manage the positioning of cameras and actors on a film set.

[1]

7 Identify **two** technical job roles that are mostly involved during **post-production**.

1. ....

2. ....

[2]

8 Which of the following **senior job roles** usually manages the schedule and budget of a project?
Tick the correct box.

☐ campaign manager

☐ creative director

☐ editor

☐ production manager

[1]

9 Identify **two** creative job roles that involve producing images to fit a **client brief**.

1. ....

2. ....

[2]

10 Identify **one** responsibility of a **campaign manager**.

....

[1]

11 Identify **two** job roles that involve writing code.

1. ....

2. ....

[2]

Purpose, Language and Tone

1   Which **one** of these options is **not** a purpose of media? Tick the correct box.

☐ Advertise

☐ Collect data

☐ Inform

☐ Persuade

[1]

2   Identify the purpose of a **textbook**.

....

[1]

3   Outline what is meant by **tone of language**.

....

....

[1]

4   Complete the sentence.

A newsreader would use f... language whereas

an influencer would use i... language.

[2]

5   State the **tone of language** that you might expect to be used in a children's TV programme.

....

[1]

6   Identify **two** media products that are commonly used for **advertising**.

1. ....

2. ....

[2]

Exam Tip

Remember to have a go at every question in the paper — don't leave an answer blank. You may not always think you know the answer, but it's better to just give it a go and write something down. After all, you've got nothing to lose.

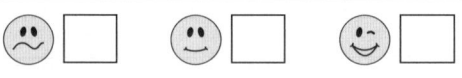

Style, Content and Layout

1 What is the meaning of the word **genre**?

....
[1]

2 What is the meaning of the term **layout**?

....
[1]

3 Identify **two** conventions of the **science fiction** genre.

1. ....

....

2. ....

....
[2]

4 Identify **two** types of **audio** used in a podcast.

1. ....

....

2. ....

....
[2]

5 Which of these is an example of **visual representation**? Tick the correct box.

☐ Background music

☐ Black and white colour scheme

☐ Cheerful tone

☐ Formal language
[1]

Audience

1   Identify **two** categories of **audience segmentation**.

1. ....

2. ....

[2]

2   Which of these best describes how a business would segment the audience to identify the **target market** for a 'high-end' product? Tick the correct box.

☐ Education

☐ Gender

☐ Income

☐ Location

[1]

3   Complete the table.

Category	Description of the category	Example of how an audience characteristic could influence product design
....	Where a person lives	People living in the countryside may be more attracted to products that focus on the natural environment.
Age	How old someone is	....

[2]

4   Identify **one** benefit of audience segmentation.

....

....

[1]

Exam Tip

When it comes to product design it's important to think about the target audience. Remember that each audience segment has different needs, so a product that suits one segment perfectly might not suit a different segment at all.

☹ ☐ ☺ ☐ ☺ ☐   Topic 2 — Factors Influencing Product Design

Client Requirements

1 Which **one** of these is **not** usually a client requirement?
Tick the correct box.

☐ Primary research methods

☐ Purpose of product

☐ Theme

☐ Timescale

[1]

2 What is the meaning of the term **timescale**?

....

....

[1]

3 A client requirement states that a new product will be used to **entertain**.
Identify what type of client requirement this is.

....

[1]

4 Complete the sentences.

The final product must align with the overall ethos and b...................................... of the client

organisation. An organisation's ethos is its v...................................... and the

things it cares about.

[2]

5 Identify **two** types of client requirement that may include information about how a product
should look.

1. ....

2. ....

[2]

6 What is the meaning of the term **house style**?

....

....

[1]

Client Brief Formats

1   Outline the meaning of the term **client brief**.

....

....

[1]

2   Which of these is **not** a detail that a client brief would usually include?
Tick the correct box.

☐ A risk assessment

☐ Information about costs

☐ Information about the product

☐ The timescales involved

[1]

3   Identify **one** difference between **formal** and **informal** briefs.

....

....

[1]

4   **Fig. 1** shows part of an email from a client.

We would like to commission you to design the cover of a new eBook, *Cosmic Quest*.

The cover of the eBook needs to meet the following requirements:
*   Fit in with the science fiction genre
*   Align with the colour scheme of our other eBooks in this series
*   Appeal to teenagers (our target audience)

As the deadline for this project is the end of May next year, we would like to see a first draft of the cover by the end of September this year.

Fig. 1

Identify **one** client brief format that this email represents.

....

[1]

5   Identify **two** parts of a client brief that might be **negotiated**.

1. ....

2. ....

[2]

Exam Tip

In the exam, remember to read the question carefully before you start writing your answer. Underline any command words like 'Identify', 'Complete' or 'State' to make sure you understand exactly what the question is asking you to do.

☹ ☐   😐 ☐   🙂 ☐   Topic 2 — Factors Influencing Product Design

Research Data and Methods

1 Which **one** of these is used for **primary** research? Tick the correct box.

☐ Books and journals

☐ Internet sites

☐ Questionnaires

☐ Television

[1]

2 State **two** advantages of using **secondary** research.

1. ....

2. ....

[2]

3 State **two** disadvantages of using **secondary** research.

1. ....

2. ....

[2]

4 Identify **one** way of collecting **quantitative** data.

....

[1]

5 Outline what is meant by **qualitative** data.

....

....

[1]

6 Identify **one** advantage and **one** disadvantage of using television content as a research source.

Advantage ....

....

Disadvantage ....

....

[2]

Topic 2 — Factors Influencing Product Design

Media Codes

1 Identify the purpose of media codes.

....

[1]

2 Which option is an example of a **technical media code**? Tick the correct box.

☐ The angle of a camera.

☐ The font size used for text on a page.

☐ The location used for a scene.

☐ The vocal intonation used by an actor.

[1]

3 Complete the sentences.

S.. codes often involve colours.

For example, the colour green often conveys something about n.. .

[2]

4 Some text on a leaflet is shown in **Fig. 1**.

get ready for
**THE SUMMER
SPECTACULAR**

Fig. 1

Identify **two** written media codes that are used in **Fig. 1**.

1. ....

2. ....

[2]

5 Identify **one** type of **audio** that can be used as a media code in a television advert.

....

[1]

Exam Tip

Make sure you know some examples of what different media codes can suggest to an audience and how they do it.
This should help you to spot media codes being used if you're shown a product in the exam — like in question 4 above.

Topic 2 — Factors Influencing Product Design

Colour, Graphics and Typography

1   The same text formatted in different ways is shown in **Fig. 1**.

A	B	C
Tap here for a receipt	Tap *here* for a receipt	T a p h e r e f o r a r e c e i p t

Fig. 1

(a)   Complete the sentence.

What letters look like is called t.. .

[1]

(b)   Identify the example in **Fig. 1** that is best described as showing emphasis.

....

[1]

2   A graphic is shown in **Fig. 2**. The colours used are yellow and black.

Fig. 2

(a)   Identify **one** way the shape of **Fig. 2** conveys meaning to the audience.

....

....

[1]

(b)   Identify **two** reasons for the choice of colours used in **Fig. 2**.

1. ....

2. ....

[2]

3   Which of the following could be used to give text a **formal** and **traditional** look?
Tick the correct box.

☐ Sans serif

☐ Bold

☐ Serif

☐ Serif sans

[1]

Topic 2 — Factors Influencing Product Design   😕☐ 😐☐ 😉☐

Lighting, Movement and Mise-en-scène

1   Identify **one** media product for which the type of **lighting** used is important.

....
                                                                                                        [1]

2   Identify the term that describes all the visual elements of a scene.

....
                                                                                                        [1]

3   Which of the following is most likely to cause an audience to feel excited? Tick the correct box.

☐   A character reading a book

☐   A slow panning shot of an empty field

☐   Characters having a quiet conversation

☐   Characters involved in a car chase
                                                                                                        [1]

4   Complete the sentence.

Mise-en-scène includes things such as the actors, c.. design,

set and l................................ .
                                                                                                        [2]

5   Outline the meaning of the term **blocking**.

....

....
                                                                                                        [1]

6   Identify **two** types of **lighting**.

1. ....

2. ....
                                                                                                        [2]

Exam Tip

Terms like mise-en-scène can be a bit tricky to get your head around, but it's important you know what they mean in case they show up in the exam. For any you aren't sure about, practise writing out a definition and repeat until it sticks.

Camera Techniques and Transitions

1 Complete the sentence.

How the director frames an actor depends on the type of shot

and the a............................... of the camera.

[1]

2 Which camera shot is more suitable for showing **emotion** on a character's face?
Tick the correct box.

☐ Close up

☐ Establishing

☐ Point of view (POV)

☐ Wide

[1]

3 Identify **one** camera technique that can be used to make a character seem less significant.

....

[1]

4 Complete the table below.

Technique	Example	Possible reason for use
Over the shoulder		So the viewer feels they are part of the conversation
Ground level		....
....		Viewers can see the layout and size of the scene, and how the characters interact

[2]

5 Identify **one** type of **camera movement**.

....

[1]

Audio

1   Identify **one** audio **transition** that can be used in a film or TV production.

    ....
                                                                                                                          [1]

2   Which **one** of these options describes how words are spoken? Tick the correct box.

    ☐ Dialogue

    ☐ Music genre

    ☐ Sound effects

    ☐ Vocal intonation
                                                                                                                          [1]

3   Complete the sentence.

    Audio added to a product in post-production includes music and s.............................. effects.
                                                                                                                          [1]

4   Identify **one** reason why a director might use silence in a scene.

    ....
                                                                                                                          [1]

5   Part of a script is shown in **Fig. 1**.

    FADE IN:
    1 INT. DAVE'S KITCHEN - DAY
    Zoe pours Mort a glass of water. Mort picks it up from the kitchen counter and then
    immediately drops it on the floor. There's a loud smash as the glass shatters into pieces.
                                      MORT
                I don't think Dave will mind. It's just a glass!
                                      ZOE
                          Oh, I think he will.
    The kitchen door swings open and Dave walks in.
                                      DAVE
                          What was that noise?

    Fig. 1

    (a) Identify what is shown as **bold** text in **Fig. 1**.

    ....
                                                                                                                          [1]

    (b) State the **job role** that involves using props to create sound effects such as breaking glass.

    ....
                                                                                                                          [1]

Exam Tip

In the exam you'll have one minute for each mark. It might help to think of this so you can use your time well.
Spending too long on one or two mark questions in Section A might mean you've not got enough time for Section B.

☺ ☐   ☺ ☐   ☺ ☐   Topic 2 — Factors Influencing Product Design

Animations and Interactivity

1 Identify **two** media products, other than AR/VR, that contain **interactive elements**.

1. ....

2. ....

[2]

2 Complete the sentence.

When a product responds to the actions of a user in some way

this is called i.. .

[1]

3 Identify **one** way **VR products** are interactive.

....

....

[1]

4 Identify **one** way that **AR products** are interactive.

....

....

[1]

5 Identify **two** ways that animation makes a website more engaging.

1. ....

2. ....

[2]

6 Which of the following is **not** an example of animation?
Tick the correct box.

☐ A scene showing a moving train from a cartoon.

☐ A scene showing a computer-generated fantasy world from a film.

☐ A clip of a reporter giving a live news report on TV.

☐ A scene showing moving plasticine animals from a children's TV programme.

[1]

Work Planning

1   Which of the following is the workplan component that allows time to deal with problems? Tick the correct box.

☐ contingencies

☐ resources

☐ spreadsheets

☐ workflow

[1]

2   Identify the workplan component that sets out the order that tasks and activities must be done.

....

[1]

3   Identify **two** components of workplans, other than **workflow**, **resources** and **contingencies**.

1. ....

2. ....

[2]

4   Identify **two** different types of resources that might be listed on a workplan.

1. ....

2. ....

[2]

5   Part of a workplan is shown in **Fig. 1**.
Identify the component labelled **A** and the phase of production labelled **B**.

Phase of Production	A	Activity	Week 1							We		
			M	T	W	T	F	S	S	M	T	W
B	Designing the product	Mood board		■								
		Mind map		■								
		Sketches			■	■						
		Visualisation diagram				■	■					
	Client meeting	Discuss planning						■				
		Finalise budget							■		■	

Fig. 1

A ....

B ....

[2]

Mind Maps and Mood Boards

1   State the **purpose** of a mind map.

....

[1]

2   Complete the sentences below.

A mind map usually starts with a key idea called the n............................... .

This is then broken down into s............................... .

[2]

3   Identify **one** piece of **software** that could be used to create a digital mind map.

....

[1]

4   Which of the following is a common feature of a **mood board**?
Tick the correct box.

☐   camera angles

☐   colour schemes

☐   connectors

☐   sub-nodes

[1]

5   Identify **one** user of a mood board in the media industry.

....

[1]

6   State **one** component that can be included in a **digital** mood
board but **not** in a **physical** mood board.

....

[1]

Topic 3 — Pre-production Planning

Planning Documents

1 Identify **two** pieces of information that should be included in an asset log.

1. ....

2. ....

[2]

2 Identify **two** types of asset that should be recorded in an asset log.

1. ....

2. ....

[2]

3 Identify **one** planning document that can be used to plan an interactive product like a website.

....

[1]

4 Which of the following can be shown by a flowchart?
Tick the correct box.

☐ assets

☐ colour schemes

☐ initial ideas

☐ processes

[1]

5 Fill in the table below by identifying what the shapes represent in a flowchart.
One row has been completed for you.

Flowchart shape	What it represents
⬭	Start or stop
◇	....
▭	....

[2]

Exam Tip

There's a bunch of planning documents you might be tested on. If you're able to pick out the best planning document for a given purpose you won't go too far wrong. Make sure you know the usual features and layout of each of them too.

Topic 3 — Pre-production Planning

Storyboards and Scripts

1 Which of the following is a storyboard used to plan?
Tick the correct box.

☐ artwork for a book cover

☐ events in a film

☐ initial ideas for a poster

☐ web page layout

[1]

2 Identify **two** job roles that are likely to use a storyboard.

1. ....

2. ....

[2]

3 Identify **two** media products that are likely to be planned using a storyboard.

1. ....

2. ....

[2]

4 Identify **two users** of a script.

1. ....

2. ....

[2]

5 Identify **one** product, other than video, that is likely to be based on a script.

....

[1]

6 Identify **one** feature of a script that is **not** a feature of a storyboard.

....

[1]

Visualisation Diagrams and Wireframes

1 Which of the following is likely to be planned using a visualisation diagram?
Tick the correct box.

☐ an eBook

☐ a film

☐ a film poster

☐ a podcast

[1]

2 Identify **two** typical components of a visualisation diagram.

1. ....

2. ....

[2]

3 Identify **two** users of visualisation diagrams.

1. ....

2. ....

[2]

4 Identify **one** product that is often planned using a wireframe layout.

....

[1]

5 Fill in the table below by identifying what each block typically represents on a wireframe layout.

Block	What it typically represents
	....
	....

[2]

Exam Tip

Some age-old advice coming up. Read the questions carefully. You might even want to underline the key words.
For example, in question 3 above, if you skim over the word 'users' and give 'uses' (purposes), then you'll get no marks.

Topic 3 — Pre-production Planning

Protecting the Individual

1   Complete the sentence.

Permission is not needed before filming in a p... place.

[1]

2   Identify who you must get permission from before filming in a private place.

....

[1]

3   Identify **one** thing an organisation must do before using a photograph of someone commercially.

....

[1]

4   Complete the sentence.

Taking photos of someone through the window of their home without their permission

is an invasion of p... .

[1]

5   Identify the term that refers to false accusations that are **written and published**.

....

[2]

6   State the name of the defamation that involves false accusations spoken by a person
and witnessed or recorded by another person.

....

[1]

7   Which of the following statements is **false**?
Tick the correct box.

☐ Organisations must tell data subjects how their personal data will be used.

☐ Organisations must keep personal data in case it is useful for something in the future.

☐ Organisations must securely store personal data.

☐ Organisations must only keep personal data for as long as necessary.

[1]

Intellectual Property

1 Identify **two** types of work that have copyright protection.

1. ....

2. ....

[2]

2 Identify **one** way of legally protecting **inventions** (e.g. a VR headset) from being copied.

....

[1]

3 Identify **two** things that can be registered as **trademarks**, other than a name.

1. ....

2. ....

[2]

4 Identify a type of **licence** that means work can be used for free under certain conditions.

....

[1]

5 Complete the sentence.

Using copyrighted work without permission for research or personal study

is known as fair d... .

[1]

6 Which of the following is **not** used as a reminder that something has copyright protection?
Tick the correct box.

☐ ©

☐ ™

☐ password

☐ watermark

[1]

7 Identify **one** possible consequence of using copyrighted material **without** permission.

....

[1]

Exam Tip

Make sure you know all the different ways that intellectual property can be protected and which method has a license attached to it. Knowing how to identify the symbols that show protection will also help you do well in the exam.

Health and Safety

1   Identify **one** thing, other than a list of risks and hazards, that a risk assessment should include.

....

[1]

2   Identify **two** common hazards in the **pre-production** phase of a media project.

1. ....

2. ....

[2]

3   Identify **two** common hazards in the **production** phase of a media project.

1. ....

2. ....

[2]

4   Identify **two** actions that can be taken to **mitigate risks** in media productions.

1. ....

2. ....

[2]

5   Complete the sentence.

A visit to a possible filming location before filming begins

is known as a location r.. .

[1]

6   Identify **one** purpose of visiting a possible filming location before filming begins.

....

[1]

Regulation, Certification and Classification

1   What does **ASA** stand for?

   ....
   [1]

2   Identify **two** reasons why an advert may be banned by the ASA.

   1.   ....

   2.   ....
   [2]

3   Which of the following does Ofcom **not** regulate?
    Tick the correct box.

   ☐   newspapers

   ☐   online video platform content

   ☐   radio programs

   ☐   TV programs
   [1]

4   Identify the organisation that assigns age certificates to films available in the UK.

   ....
   [1]

5   Identify **one** type of content that will result in a film being assigned a higher age rating.

   ....
   [1]

6   State the type of product **PEGI** provides age ratings for.

   ....
   [1]

7   Identify the region PEGI operates in.

   ....
   [1]

Exam Tip

Wrote completely the wrong word? No problem. Just put a line through the wrong word and write the correct one next to it, like this: ~~Lagos~~ Logo. It's a good idea to check your answers through at the end for silly mistakes too.

😐 ☐   🙂 ☐   😃 ☐   Topic 3 — Pre-production Planning

Distribution Platforms

1 Which **one** of the following is a **physical** distribution platform?
Tick the correct box.

☐ App

☐ CD/DVD

☐ Interactive TV

☐ Multimedia

[1]

2 (a) Identify the **physical platform** shown in **Fig. 1** below.

Fig. 1

....
[1]

(b) Identify **one** advantage of a restaurant using the physical platform shown in **Fig. 1**.

....

....
[1]

3 Identify **two** common **online distribution platforms** for videos.

1. ....

2. ....
[2]

4 Identify **one** advantage of using **online platforms** to distribute media products.

....

....
[1]

Distribution Media

1   Complete the sentence.

Media can be distributed using p.. products such as CDs and DVDs.

[1]

2   (a)   Identify **one** advantage of using a **DVD** to distribute a film.

....

....

[1]

(b)   Identify **one** disadvantage of using a **DVD** to distribute a film.

....

....

[1]

3   (a)   Identify the physical media device shown in **Fig. 2**.

Fig. 2

....

[1]

(b)   Identify **one** disadvantage of the physical media device shown in **Fig. 2**.

....

....

[1]

4   Identify **two** examples of media content that can be distributed as **paper-based products**.

1. ....

2. ....

[2]

Exam Tip

Sometimes exam questions include diagrams or images. Don't let this throw you off — just look at them carefully and make sure that you understand what they're trying to show. It might be useful to highlight any important parts.

Topic 4 — Distribution Considerations

File Compression

1 Complete the sentences.

One reason that files get compressed is to reduce the file s ....

Another reason is to reduce the time it takes to u.................................. the files

to an online platform.

[2]

2 Complete the sentence.

Compression that permanently deletes part of a file is called

l.................................. compression.

[1]

3 Identify the type of compression you should use when uploading videos to a **streaming website**.

....

[1]

4 Identify **one** scenario where you must use **lossless** compression.

....

[1]

5 Which **one** of the following statements does **not** describe **lossy** compression?
Tick the correct box.

☐ It reduces file size but causes a reduction in quality.

☐ It's often used when archiving files.

☐ It's the type of compression that reduces file size the most.

☐ When a file is decompressed it doesn't look the same as the original file.

[1]

Image Files

1 Complete the sentences.

A v............................ image uses coordinates, colours and curves to represent the shapes.

A b.. image is made up of a grid of pixels.

[2]

2 Which of the following images is most likely to be saved as a **raster image**?
Tick the correct box.

☐ A cartoon character

☐ A logo for a company

☐ A photo of a landscape

☐ An icon for a home page

[1]

3 Identify **two** effects of increasing the **DPI** of an image.

1. ....

2. ....

[2]

4 Complete the table below.

File format	Vector or bitmap?
.tiff	bitmap
.jpg	....
.svg	....

[2]

5 Complete the sentence.

An image is 4000 pixels wide and 2000 pixels tall.

This is called its pixel d.. .

[1]

Audio Files

1   Identify **two** properties of an audio file that determine the **quality** of a recording.

     1. ....

     2. ....

                                                                      [2]

2   Identify the units of data used to store **audio samples**.

     ....

                                                                      [1]

3   Complete the sentence.

     Sample rate is the number of samples taken each s............................... .

                                                                      [1]

4   Identify **two** effects of reducing the **bit depth** of an audio file.

     1. ....

     2. ....

                                                                      [2]

5   State **one** situation in which audio files need to be compressed.

     ....

                                                                      [1]

6   Identify the type of compression used in a **.mp3** file.

     ....

                                                                      [1]

7   Identify **one** uncompressed audio file format.

     ....

                                                                      [1]

Moving Image Files

1 Identify **one** media product that uses **moving images**.

....

[1]

2 Which of the following resolutions is **lowest**?
Tick the correct box.

☐ 4K

☐ 8K

☐ HD

☐ UHD

[1]

3 State what the letter **D** represents in HD and UHD.

....

[1]

4 Complete the sentence.

The resolution of a moving image file relates to the number of p.................................

in each f................................. .

[2]

5 Identify **two** moving image file formats.

1. ....

2. ....

[2]

6 Complete the sentence.

A disadvantage of using a higher frame rate is a larger

f................................. s................................. .

[1]

Exam Tip

There's no need to panic if you tick a box in a multiple choice question and then realise that you've made a mistake.
Just make sure that you clearly and neatly cross out the incorrect answer before ticking the correct box instead.

Mixed Practice

1   **Fig. 1** shows a printed graphic product.

Norman Worstle

Vote for me,
vote for
the planet

Fig. 1

(a)   Which of the following is the main **purpose** of the graphic product in **Fig. 1**?
       Tick the correct box.

☐ educate

☐ entertain

☐ influence

☐ inform

[1]

(b)   The main colour used in the graphic product shown in **Fig. 1** is green.
       Identify the type of **media code** the use of the colour green demonstrates.

....

[1]

(c)   Identify **one** creative job role that is likely to have been involved in the production of the
       graphic product in **Fig. 1**.

....

[1]

(d)   Identify **two** types of **planning document** likely to have been used in
       creating the graphic product in **Fig. 1**.

1. ....

2. ....

[2]

Mixed Practice

2 Which of the following file types has a **sample rate**?
Tick the correct box.

☐ audio

☐ bitmap

☐ moving image

☐ vector

[1]

3 Identify **two advantages** of using files compressed by **lossy** compression
rather than **lossless** compression.

1. ....

2. ....

[2]

4 Which of the following types of media product should have a minimum resolution of 72 PPI?
Tick the correct box.

☐ audio recordings

☐ digital images

☐ moving images

☐ print products

[1]

5 Identify the type of content monitored by the ASA.

....

[1]

6 Identify **one** camera shot which is used to show the location of the following scenes.

....

[1]

Exam Tip

The questions on these pages aren't neatly arranged in topic order — you have to be able to dredge up facts from any part of the course, just like in the exam. If you're finding a particular question tough you should check it out in your notes.

☹ ☐   😐 ☐   😊 ☐

Mixed Practice

7   Which of the following types of **brief** allows the designer to respond with their thoughts after receiving an initial brief?

Tick the correct box.

☐ formal

☐ informal

☐ negotiated

☐ written

[1]

8   Identify **two disadvantages** of distributing media as paper-based products.

1. ....

2. ....

[2]

9   Identify **one** document which is intended to keep people involved in a media production as safe as possible.

....

[1]

10   Which of the following is **horror** an example of?

Tick the correct box.

☐ convention

☐ genre

☐ mise-en-scène

☐ tone

[1]

11   Complete the sentence.

Key points in a project which may have their own deadlines are known

as m... .

[1]

Section B Questions

Section B is the **second section** of the written exam. It's worth **60** out of the 70 marks available in the exam — so it's **pretty important**.

See page 2 for information about Section A, which contains the other 10 marks.

Some of the questions in Section B will be similar to those in Section A — so you'll still get **1–2 mark questions** that use command words like '**Identify**'.

However, there will also be **longer questions** that use command words like '**Describe**' and '**Explain**'.

There will also be **one 6-mark question** (see page 41) and **two 9-mark questions**. One of the 9-markers will ask you to **evaluate** or **discuss** someone else's work (see page 42). The other will ask you to make an **improved version** of someone else's work, and to **justify** your improvements (page 43).

Section B Questions are All Based on a Scenario

At the start of Section B, you'll be introduced to a **scenario**. This will generally be based on a made-up **organisation** in the media industry. Every exam will have **one** scenario, and it's **different** every time. Many of the questions will need you to think about this scenario and **use it** in your answer.

	Section B	
The scenario is provided at the start of Section B. More details will be added later on in the section.		It can be useful to underline what seems like key information in the scenario.

Creative Coders make <u>websites</u> for clients. They are involved in the whole process of creating websites, from the initial <u>design</u> and creating the <u>graphics</u>, to actually <u>coding</u> the web pages.

They are currently involved in a project to create a website for a <u>primary school</u>. The website needs to be ready for the start of the <u>school year</u>, which is in <u>three months</u> time.

You have recently been hired as the <u>creative director</u> for Creative Coders.

1   Identify **two** creative job roles that will be needed by Creative Coders.

1. ...*web designer*...

2. ...*graphic designer*...

[2]

Question 1 needs to you pick out details from the scenario. The scenario mentions designing websites (which is done by a web designer) and creating graphics (done by a graphic designer or illustrator) — these are both creative jobs.

2   Identify **one** pre-production document that could be used to design the website.

......*wireframe layout*...

[1]

For this question, you need to think about what would be sensible — an answer isn't given in the scenario.

Not all documents are appropriate for the task in the scenario (designing websites). For example, there's no mention of video or audio, so a script or storyboard isn't sensible.

Describe and Explain Questions

'Describe' Questions Need Some Detail in their Answers

Questions with the '**describe**' command word need you to write **a sentence or more**.
They often focus on the **purpose** of something or **how** something is done.

Some 'describe' questions require a **fairly short** answer:

3 (a) Describe **one** client requirement that Creative Coders needs to follow.

...The website must be done by the start of the school year, which is in two months.............

[1]

Even for a 1 mark 'describe' question you need to write a sentence, not just a word or two.

Use the number of marks available to decide how many points to make.

Others need you to make **more than one point**.
Try to **connect up** the points in your answer.

Not all Section B questions will be about the scenario. If the scenario isn't mentioned, you don't need to include it.

(b) Describe how a **formal** client brief can be developed.

...The client and a designer could have a meeting in which the terms of the brief are negotiated.......

...Afterwards, notes from the meeting could be sent around to summarise what was agreed............

...Then a legal contract setting out the terms could be written and signed by both parties.................

[3]

Words like 'afterwards' and 'then' have been used to link the points together.

Try to make one point for each mark available — in this case 3. Putting each point in a separate sentence can make them clearer.

'Explain' Questions Focus on the Reasons For Something

If you're asked to **explain** something, you need to focus on **why** something is how it is.

It might help to imagine the examiner knows nothing and you are teaching them.

4 Explain why a radio station must follow Ofcom regulations.

...Ofcom are the regulator for the radio industry. Therefore, they.......

...have the power to fine radio stations which don't follow the rules...............

[2]

Linking words like 'therefore' make it clear you are explaining something.

A good way to structure your answer is to make a point, and then expand on it.

You are asked to explain **one** right in this question, so state **one** right and then expand on it. Don't add a second right — you won't get a mark for it.

5 Explain **one** right that data subjects have over their personal data.

...They may request that their data is deleted. The organisation.............

...must delete it or they may be fined...................

[2]

Answering 6-Mark Questions

Watch out for the 6-Mark Question

The **6-mark question** requires longer answers and is marked a bit **differently** to shorter questions. For shorter questions, you get a mark for **each correct point** you make. However, 6-mark questions (and also the two 9-markers) are marked using '**levels**' that rate your answer as 'high', 'mid', or 'low'. You can judge how long your answer needs to be by looking at the number of dotted lines but the examiner will be looking at the **overall quality** of your answer.

High-level answers contain a range of **connected points**, which are **explained** or **described**, and use **key terminology**.

An Example of a Strong Answer to a 6-Mark Question...

6   Explain **two** benefits of using compression on images that are used on a website.

One benefit is that the images will take up less storage space on the computer running the website (the server). This is because compression reduces file size, so the images take up less storage space. This is good because the computer then has more space to store other files.

Another benefit is that it will take less time to download the images when the website loads. This is because the file is smaller, so less data has to be transferred. This benefits the user as they don't have to wait as long for the website to load.

[6]

> The two benefits are separated into different paragraphs.

> Each benefit has been explained and clearly shows why compression is used on images for a website.

> Using the correct terminology is a good way to show off your knowledge. E.g. the terms 'storage space', 'server', 'file size' and 'download' have been used here. Writing "compression makes them smaller" would be a poor use of terminology because it's too vague — it's not clear what 'them' are and what part of 'them' is made smaller.

... and an Example of a Weaker Answer

7   Describe **three** ways camera techniques can be used by a director to convey meaning, create impact and engage audiences.

If characters are running, the camera could move to follow them.

This could make the audience feel they are part of the action.

Using a low angle can also make a character seem powerful.

[6]

> This answer would only get a few marks. Only two ways of using camera techniques are identified and only one of these is expanded on.

> A stronger answer might have described the second point about low angles more and then included a third described point. E.g. "If a character was showing strong emotion, such as rage, a camera could zoom into their face so audiences focus on this emotion and perhaps relate to it".

> If you know key terms, this is the time to use them. For example, you might add that a 'track and dolly' could be used to allow the camera to move. You could also say that a low camera angle might allow a 'tilt up'.

Answering 9-Mark Questions

One 9-Mark Question Asks You to Evaluate Someone's Work

This 9-mark question asks you to **discuss the suitability** of some work.
When answering this question, make sure you:

- Identify the **good parts** of the work and say **why** they are good.
- Identify the **bad parts** of the work and say **why** they are problems.
- Make **suggestions** for how to **improve** the work and **explain** each suggestion.

> The work you're presented with could be a pre-production document (e.g. a mood board or flowchart), or a completed product (such as a comic or a book cover).

Have a look at this **9-mark 'discuss'** question and example answer.

---

8   A web designer has produced the wireframe layout shown in **Fig. 1**.

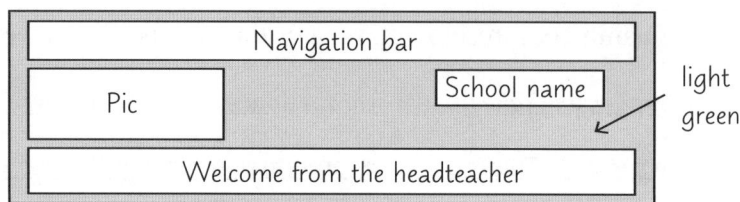

Fig. 1

Discuss the suitability of this wireframe layout for the web developer.

Marks will be awarded for:

- Suggesting changes that improve the wireframe layout.
- Explaining how these changes improve the effectiveness of the wireframe layout for the web developer.

> Think about the purpose and the target audience of the work. In this case, the purpose is to tell the web developer what to make. So your answer must be about how well you think this document will do this — the web developer is the audience.

The wireframe layout shows the main components of the webpage so that the web developer can put them in the correct positions. Each component also has a label, so the web developer knows what each one should be. The sizes of components may not be realistic though — e.g. the 'welcome' text is squeezed into a very small area. A wireframe layout should show sizes accurately. Some labels are not detailed enough, for example 'pic' is very vague. A better label would be e.g. 'school logo' or 'photo of a pupil'. Other details are missing, e.g. the navigation bar has no buttons shown, so the developer won't know what links to put in. While the one annotation about the background colour is helpful, the wireframe layout needs more annotations telling the developer what to do. For example, the wireframe layout would be improved by annotations such as 'blue buttons with the font in white' with an arrow going towards the navigation bar.

[9]

> High-level answers use correct terminology, e.g. 'components', 'buttons' and 'links'.

Exam Skills 2

Answering 9-Mark Questions

The Other 9-Mark Question Asks You to Improve a Document

You'll be shown a **pre-production document** and asked to **create a better version** of it.

Pre-production documents are used to generate ideas, design, and plan the products, e.g. mind maps or flow charts.

For this question, you need to:

- Draw the **improved version** of the document. Make it like the examples you have seen throughout the course — use the **same components** and **layout conventions**.

- Add **annotations** with arrows to **explain** the improvements you've added and **why** they help.

Here's a 9-mark **'create'** question and example answer:

9   One requirement for Creative Coders is that the website must promote the school's Year 6 production. A banner advertisement needs to be made for parents to see.

Fig. 2 shows a draft visualisation diagram for this advertisement made by one of the teachers.

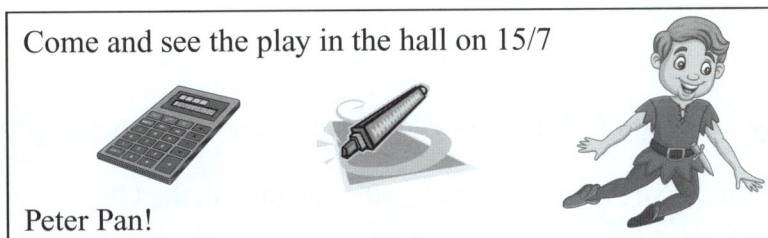

Come and see the play in the hall on 15/7

Peter Pan!

Fig. 2

Don't ignore the draft version. You need to think about what isn't effective about it, so you can include clear improvements in yours.

This draft is the right shape for the banner, but some issues include:

- The title is far too small and isn't easy to spot in the bottom corner.
- The calculator and pen images don't fit the theme.
- There are no annotations to help explain how the advert should look.

Create an improved version of the visualisation diagram.

Marks will be awarded for:

- Relevant components and conventions
- Layout
- Annotations that explain how the improvements better meet the school's requirements.

You don't get marks for artistic flair, but you may want to do quick sketches or shading. Or, just add boxes with labels — this isn't GCSE Art, after all.

Add annotations explaining your changes — put these within the answer box but off to the sides.

The title is big and bold and the first thing you see. It is placed top left to follow convention.

Photos of children make it clear this is a school production.

Dark green text

Black text

PETER PAN

In the school hall
On 15/7 only!
The Year 6s can't wait to see you there.

Photo of girl and boy performing on stage

Peter Pan facing this way

Light green background (fits the theme)

The black text will be clearly visible against the light green background.

All text is aligned left to keep it organised and make it easy to read.

A message that seems personal will help persuade parents to come.

The picture in the draft was facing away. Flipping it means it looks towards the text. This more engaging and frames the banner.

Nostalgic Flicks

Nostalgic Flicks is a cinema that only shows films released before 2000.
For the upcoming summer holiday, they are going to use one of their
screens to show films aimed at children between 8 and 13 years old.

Nostalgic Flicks has hired you to oversee a marketing campaign to inform people
about this summer programme of films for 8 to 13 year olds. The campaign should
involve a magazine advertisement and a video to be posted on social media.

1   The summer film programme is aimed at a specific audience.

Identify **one audience segment** that the summer programme targets.

....

[1]

2   Nostalgic Flicks need to display information about how films being shown have been classified.

(a)   Identify the **organisation** which is responsible for classifying films in the UK.

....

[1]

(b)   Describe **one** kind of **classification** films are given.

....

....

[2]

3   A director has been hired to direct a video for Nostalgic Flicks to use on social media.

Describe **three** responsibilities the **director** would have while working on this project.

1. ....

....

2. ....

....

3. ....

....

[3]

Nostalgic Flicks

4 To decide which films to show in the cinema, the Nostalgic Flicks manager does research online. She uses a search engine to look for successful children's films first shown between 1980 and 2000.

(a) Identify the type of **research** that this online research is classed as.

....

[1]

(b) Justify your answer to part (a).

....

....

....

[1]

5 After completing her research, the manager has a list containing the name of every children's film she found that met her criteria.

(a) Identify the type of **research data** that this list of names is classed as.

....

[1]

(b) Describe a **primary research method** the manager could have used to find this information.

....

....

....

....

[2]

6 The manager of Nostalgic Flicks wants to keep track of how many people attend each film shown during the summer programme.

Identify the type of **research data** this information would be classed as.

....

[1]

Exam Tip

Now for some handy advice. If you make a mistake when writing an answer to a question just put a line through any bits that you don't want marking. Make sure you do this carefully though — it needs to be crystal clear to the marker.

Nostalgic Flicks

7   **Fig. 1** shows a draft advertisement made by a member of staff at Nostalgic Flicks cinema before you joined the project. The plan was to publish it in a local lifestyle magazine aimed at adults. The member of staff has labelled the colours the advertisement would have when printed.

Fig. 1

Discuss the suitability of this magazine advertisement.

Marks will be awarded for:

- Considering to what extent the advert is fit for purpose.
- Suggesting changes that would improve the advert.
- Explaining why the changes you have suggested would improve the advert.

....

....

....

....

....

....

....

....

....

....

....

....

....

....

[9]

Nostalgic Flicks

8   You have decided to make a workplan for the Nostalgic Flicks project.
Fig. 2 below is an extract from the workplan.

Tasks	Activities	Week 1							Week 2							Week 3				
		M	T	W	T	F	S	S	M	T	W	T	F	S	S	M	T	W	T	F
Plan marketing campaign	Initial client meetings	▓	▓																	
	Research target audience			▓	▓	▓			▓											
	Mood boards and sketches										▓	▓	▓			▓	▓	▓		
	Client meeting																		▓	

Fig. 2

(a)   Identify **three** components of a workplan that are included in **Fig. 2**.

1. ....

2. ....

3. ....
[3]

(b)   Identify **one** component of a workplan that is not included in **Fig. 2**.

....
[1]

(c)   Explain **two** advantages of using workplans.

1. ....

....

....

....

2. ....

....

....

....
[4]

Exam Tip
If a question asks you to 'identify' something it'll only need a short answer. This might be a single word or a few words. You might be asked to identify more than one thing — look out for a number in **bold** in the question. Time for a tea?

Nostalgic Flicks

9 Nostalgic Flicks decide that the social media video will be compressed.

    (a) Explain **one** benefit of compressing the video for use on social media.

....

....

[2]

    (b) Identify which **type** of file compression is most likely to be used for the video uploaded to social media.

....

[1]

    (c) Explain why the type of compression you identified in part (b) is unlikely to be used on the films to be shown in the cinema.

....

....

....

[2]

10 The social media video is exported in high definition (HD). However, the films selected for the summer programme will be shown at the cinema in standard definition (SD).

Explain why the films are in **SD**.

....

....

....

....

[2]

11 Nostalgic Flicks also want to advertise their summer children's films on a poster.

    (a) Identify **one job role** that might be involved in creating the poster.

....

[1]

    (b) Explain **one** element that could go on the poster to attract Nostalgic Flicks's **target audience**.

....

....

....

[2]

Nostalgic Flicks

12 **Fig. 3** is a draft storyboard for the social media platform. The aim of the storyboard is to provide the director with all the information they need to make a video.

FRAME 1		
Picture of popcorn	Video of an older teenager walking in and then sitting down in a cinema seat	Shot of the cinema screen playing a film
FRAME 2	**FRAME 3**	**FRAME 4**
Some information written on a clapperboard about the promo	Actor talks about the film	Screen fades to black

Fig. 3

Create an improved version of the storyboard shown in **Fig. 3**.

Marks will be awarded for:

• Relevant components and conventions used

• Layout

• Annotations that explain how your improvements will do a better job of meeting the needs of the director and the requirements of the Nostalgic Flicks campaign.

[9]

Exam Tip

In this 9-mark question you need to do some drawing. Your drawings only need to be sketches though, so don't worry about them being masterpieces. They just need to be clear enough that they show what's going on in each scene.

Nostalgic Flicks

13 Nostalgic Flicks screens films that have been made by the film industry. Film is an example of a traditional media sector.

(a) Identify **two traditional media sectors**, other than film.

1. ....

2. ....

[2]

(b) Describe **two** ways that the **film industry** is evolving as a result of **digital technology**.

1. ....

....

....

....

2. ....

....

....

....

[4]

14 Many of the films shown by Nostalgic Flicks use special effects (SFX).

(a) Outline what **special effects** are and give **one** example of how they can be used in a film.

....

....

....

[2]

Films can also make use of visual effects (VFX).

(b) Outline what **visual effects** are and give **one** example of how they can be used in a film.

....

....

....

....

[2]

Nostalgic Flicks

15 As part of your role working with Nostalgic Flicks, you are overseeing the production of a magazine advertisement.

(a) An **asset log** may be used in this process. Identify **one** use of an asset log.

....

....

[1]

The magazine advert will contain photographs taken by employees of the cinema.

(b) Describe how **photographs** used in the advert are protected from being used by other people.

....

....

....

....

[2]

A graphic designer is hired to work on the magazine advert.

(c) Explain **two** ways that a **graphic designer** could contribute to the creation of the magazine advert.

....

....

....

....

....

....

....

....

....

....

....

[6]

Exam Tip

A creative role like a graphic designer is involved in lots of different tasks in all three production phases. You need to know plenty of examples of these different tasks. Make sure you can do the same thing for senior and technical roles too.

Rooftop Rangers

Parkour is a sport that involves running, jumping and climbing through a built-up environment using the obstacles encountered to help you. Often this is done at a fast pace and at height.

Rooftop Rangers are a newly-formed parkour group that perform stunts for film and television. Their work mostly appeals to teenagers and adults who like extreme sports.

You've been hired to be the group's campaign manager to help them develop their brand. They need a logo to represent their group. Rooftop Rangers also need to come up with a parkour sequence which is to be filmed as part of a scene in an action film.

1 Media producers need to be aware of the intended purpose of the product and also the target audience.

(a) The purpose of the action film is to entertain viewers.
Identify **two** other possible **purposes** of media products.

1. ....

2. ....

[2]

(b) (i) Explain what is meant by **audience segmentation**.

....

....

[1]

(ii) Identify **one** category of audience segmentation.

....

[1]

(c) Explain **two benefits** of audience segmentation.

1. ....

....

....

....

2. ....

....

....

....

[4]

Exam Tip

Wahoo! Another scenario to get your head around. Take your time to read it through and underline any keywords. It's important to soak in all the info as the questions that follow will often need answers that are tailored to the scenario.

Rooftop Rangers

2 Before you were hired as their campaign manager, the Rooftop Rangers parkour group created a mood board to help them come up with ideas for their logo.

(a) Identify **one hardware** device and **one** type of **software** that can be used to create a digital mood board.

Hardware: ....

Software: ....

[2]

(b) **Fig. 1** shows the content that Rooftop Rangers considered putting on their digital mood board.

1. A photo of a trainer	2. A cartoon of a trainer	3. A photo showing the colour of concrete	4. A photo of rugby players
5. A photo of a young woman jumping over a wall	6. A photo showing the texture of grass	7. A cartoon of a young man jumping down	8. A photo showing the colour of water
	Times New Roman Bell MT Baskerville Old Face		**Futura LT Pro** Arial Agency FB
9. A logo of a competitor parkour group	10. Sample text of traditional fonts	11. A logo of a nearby cricket club	12. Sample text of modern fonts
13. A photo of skyscrapers	14. A fast-paced song	15. A cartoon of a sofa	16. Sound of an aeroplane taking off

Fig. 1

Rooftop Rangers

Fig. 2 shows a version of the digital mood board that was created by the Rooftop Rangers group.

PITCHWORTH
PARK

CRICKET CLUB

Fig. 2

Create an improved version of the mood board shown by **Fig. 2** using content from **Fig. 1**.

You do not need to draw the content. Show the content that you are using by giving the written label of each piece of content from **Fig. 1**. You can also add suggestions of your own, e.g. colours.

Marks will be awarded for:

* Relevant components used

* Layout

* Explaining how the changes you suggest will improve the effectiveness of the mood board as a source of inspiration for the logo.

[9]

Rooftop Rangers

3 Rooftop Rangers used newspapers and magazines to do some secondary research.

Describe **one** advantage and **one** disadvantage of **researching** using magazines and newspapers.

....

....

....

....

[4]

4 Rooftop Rangers are deciding on their logo and want it to reflect the kind of work they do. Part of this involves deciding on the typography used in the logo. **Fig. 3** shows two versions of the group's name in the same font size.

Rooftop Rangers	Rooftop Rangers

Fig. 3

Identify **two** differences between the examples used in **Fig. 3**.

1. ....

2. ....

[2]

5 Properties of the image file for Rooftop Rangers' logo will need to be decided.

(a) (i) Identify what **DPI** stands for.

....

[1]

(ii) Identify what **PPI** stands for.

....

[1]

One option is to save the logo in a vector file format.

(b) Explain **one disadvantage** of using vector image files.

....

....

....

[2]

Exam Tip

Even though question 5 (b) asks for one thing it's worth two marks — to get both you need to give a disadvantage (1 mark) **and** explain it (1 mark). Always check the number of marks a question is worth before you start writing.

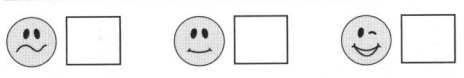

Rooftop Rangers

6 **Fig. 4** is a visualisation diagram of the logo that the Rooftop Rangers group have come up with. This will be used by a graphic designer to create the final logo.

Fig. 4

Discuss the suitability of this visualisation diagram for the graphic designer.

Marks will be awarded for:

- Considering to what extent the visualisation diagram is fit for purpose.
- Suggesting changes that would improve the visualisation diagram.
- Explaining why the changes you have suggested would improve the visualisation diagram.

....

....

....

....

....

....

....

....

....

....

....

....

....

....

....

....

[9]

Rooftop Rangers

7   During the pre-production phase of the film, the production manager carries out a location recce.

Describe what a **location recce** is.

....

....

[1]

8   As part of their role, the production manager investigates possible hazards.

     (a)   Describe **three** possible **hazards** that could affect the filming of the
Rooftop Rangers action sequence.

        1. ....

        ....

        2. ....

        ....

        3. ....

        ....

[3]

The production manager want to mitigate hazards.

     (b)   Complete the **risk assessment** table shown below using **one** of the hazards you identified in
your answer to part (a).

Hazard	....
Potential consequence	....
Way to mitigate hazard	....

[2]

Exam Tip

When completing a table make sure you understand what needs to go in each row or column before writing anything.

Rooftop Rangers

9 Rooftop Rangers will work with the film director to plan their action sequence. It will involve the parkour group performing stunts while chasing the enemy across the roofs of high-rise buildings.

Explain how camera techniques and lighting can be used to engage the audience throughout the action sequence.

....

....

....

....

....

....

....

....

[6]

10 Films can be distributed on physical media.

(a) (i) Describe what is meant by **physical media**.

....

....

[1]

(ii) Identify **one** example of **physical media**.

....

[1]

The film that the Rooftop Rangers are featuring in will be distributed using online platforms.

(b) Describe **two** reasons why a film might be distributed using **online platforms**.

1. ....

....

2. ....

....

[2]

Rooftop Rangers

11 As part of the film's promotion, a 'behind the scenes' video will be made with the members of Rooftop Rangers talking about how their scene was filmed. The members of the group will need to consider the tone of language they use.

Explain **one** way the **tone** of language they use may need to be adapted for this video.

....

....

....

....

[2]

12 An audio technician will need to be involved in the production of this 'behind the scenes' video.

(a) Describe **two** responsibilities of the **audio technician** working on this video.

....

....

....

....

....

....

....

[4]

(b) Describe **two** camera techniques that might be used for filming this video.

....

....

....

....

....

....

[4]

Exam Tip

It's important that you're familiar with common camera techniques and how they're used. Look up different shots, angles and movements online and watch some examples. There are loads of film clips available online to help with this.

CPG Labs

CPG Labs are a software development company. They are working on a new product called 'Rate Your Restaurants' that allows customers to anonymously rate the restaurants they eat at.

Rate Your Restaurants needs to work on several different physical platforms. On the mobile app, there will be an augmented reality (AR) feature which enables users to use their smartphone to see the ratings of restaurants around them in an engaging way.

1   CPG Labs can be considered a new media company.

Identify the **sector** within new media that CPG Labs is part of.

....

[1]

2   Augmented reality is a similar media product to virtual reality (VR).

(a)   Describe what **AR** and **VR** are.

AR: ....

....

VR: ....

....

[2]

(b)   Identify **one** media product, other than augmented reality and virtual reality, that could be used as part of the app.

....

[1]

(c)   Identify **two physical platforms**, other than mobile devices (e.g. smartphones), that Rate Your Restaurants could be used with.

1. ....

2. ....

[2]

3   The team at CPG Labs need to consider the pixel dimension of each digital image that they create for Rate Your Restaurants.

Explain **one** way that the **physical platform** used might affect the **pixel dimension** required.

....

....

....

....

[2]

CPG Labs

4   **Fig.1** shows a flow chart made by a senior employee at CPG Labs. The flow chart is meant to be used by the app creators so they can understand how to create the ratings part of the app.

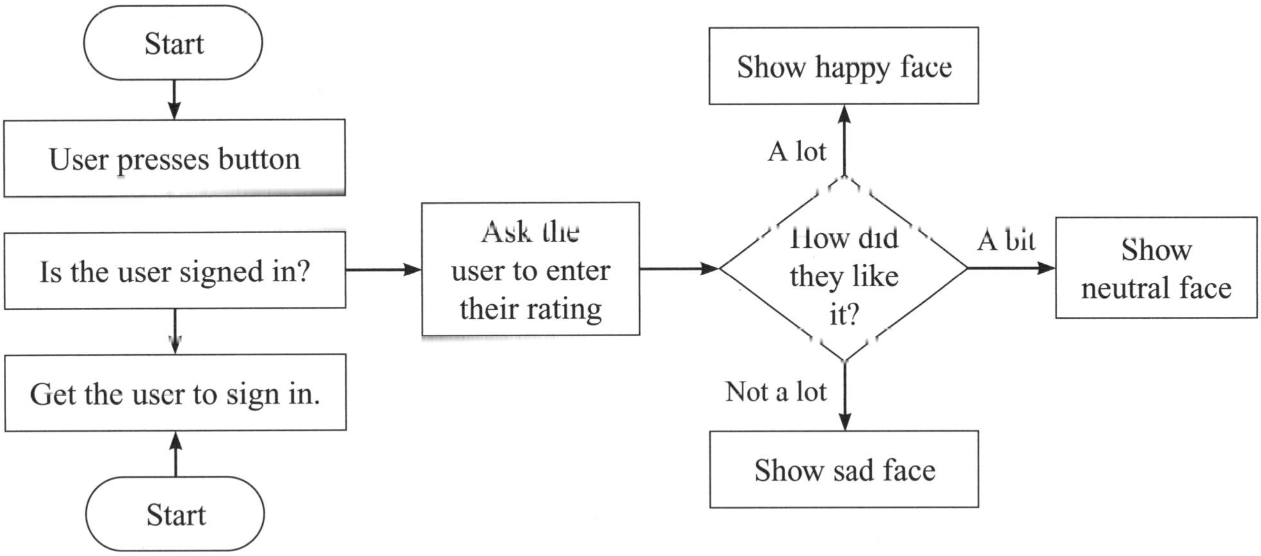

Fig. 1

Discuss the suitability of this flow chart for the app creators.

Marks will be awarded for:

- Considering to what extent the flow chart is fit for purpose.
- Suggesting changes that would improve the flow chart.
- Explaining why the changes you have suggested would improve the flow chart.

....

....

....

....

....

....

....

....

....

....

....

[9]

Exam Tip

When a question has a diagram make sure you look over it carefully before you start writing your answer. You could even underline important parts. The diagram is there for a reason and you should be talking about it in your answer.

CPG Labs

5 CPG Labs hire a content creator to support their efforts to promote their products.

(a) Describe the role of a **content creator**.

....

....

[1]

The content creator is given a client brief by CPG Labs that contains requirements for a short video they would like them to record.

(b) Describe **two** requirements that could be in the **client brief** given to the **content creator**.

Requirement 1 ....

....

....

....

Requirement 2 ....

....

....

....

[4]

The content creator is asked to provide a script for approval by CPG Labs before beginning production.

(c) Identify **two** components you would expect to be in the **script**, other than dialogue.

1. ....

2. ....

[2]

(d) Describe **one technical code** that the content creator could use in their production.

....

....

....

[2]

CPG Labs

6   It is important that organisations like CPG Labs consider legal issues that affect media.

(a)   Identify **one** legal measure that a **media organisation** can take to protect their brand name.

....

[1]

CPG Labs would like to use photos that their customers have taken at restaurants for a promotional campaign.

(b)   Explain what they need to do to use these photos legally.

....

....

....

[2]

CPG Labs want to store personal data about their customers such as their name, phone number, e-mail address and location.

(c)   Explain what **rights** their customers have over the **collection**, **use** and **storage** of their personal data.

....

....

....

....

....

....

....

....

....

....

....

[6]

Exam Tip

Try not to be vague in your answers, especially with questions where you need to 'Explain' something. It's always a good idea to be as specific as you can, with clear and relevant examples to back up the points you're making.

CPG Labs

7   A range of different job roles exist at media companies such as CPG Labs.

(a) Identify **two creative job roles** that might exist at a large media company.

1. ....

2. ....

[2]

(b) For each of the **two** creative job roles you identified, describe **one** main responsibility and identify the phase of production they're mainly involved in.

1. ....

....

....

2. ....

....

....

[4]

A person in a senior role at CPG Labs is the creative director.

(c) Describe **three** responsibilities the **creative director** at CPG Labs would be likely to have.

1. ....

....

....

2. ....

....

....

3. ....

....

....

[3]

CPG Labs

8 CPG Labs plans to show an advert on television when their mobile app is launched.

(a) Identify the organisation responsible for **regulating adverts** in the UK.

....

[1]

(b) Describe the role of the organisation you named in your answer to (a).

....

....

....

....

[2]

An employee points out that CPG Labs will need to be careful to avoid defamation in the television advert.

(c) Outline what **defamation** is and why it is a risk in this situation.

....

....

....

....

[2]

A focus group is used to conduct research when planning the television advert.

(d) Describe **one** disadvantage of using a **focus group**.

....

....

....

....

....

[2]

Exam Tip

There are a few technical terms covered on this page. (Who knew a TV advert could be so complicated, eh?) If you didn't feel confident about regulation, defamation or focus groups give them a good going over before it's exam time.

CPG Labs

9   **Fig. 2** is part of the client brief for the mobile app.

> The app should be accessible to a wide variety of users so the font(s) and colour scheme used should make any text easy to read. This aligns with the company's core value of inclusivity. The graphics used must be related to food. The app must also have a navigation bar at the top of each page to go between the different pages: 'Home', 'Rate a Restaurant' and 'See Restaurants' (this page has the AR feature). The 'Rate a Restaurant' page must contain two text boxes for user inputs (one for the restaurant name and another for its rating) and a button to submit a review. When the button is tapped a sound effect will play. The 'See Restaurants' page should contain a description of the AR feature and a box in which the AR camera view will be displayed.

Fig. 2

(a)   Identify **one client requirement** that relates to the content of the media product.

....

....

[1]

(b)   Identify **one** client requirement that relates to the company's **ethos**.

....

....

[1]

(c)   State an example of a **sound effect** that could play when a user submits a review in the app.

....

[1]

Fig. 3 shows a draft wireframe layout that was created based on this client brief. This will be used by the app creators during production of the mobile app.

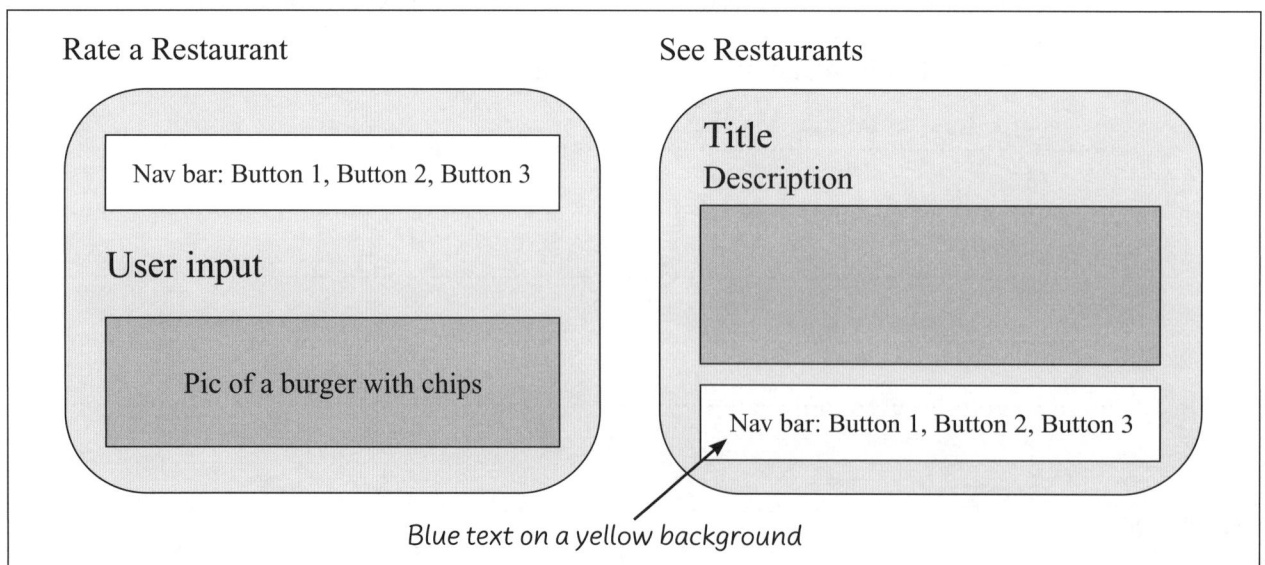

Rate a Restaurant   See Restaurants

Nav bar: Button 1, Button 2, Button 3

User input

Pic of a burger with chips

Title
Description

Nav bar: Button 1, Button 2, Button 3

Blue text on a yellow background

Fig. 3

CPG Labs

(d)   Create an improved version of the draft wireframe layout in **Fig. 3**.
      Your layout should only include the 'Rate a Restaurant' and 'See Restaurants' pages.
      Marks will be awarded for:

* Relevant components and conventions used
* Layout
* Annotations that explain how the improvements better meet the requirements of the client and also explain more clearly to the app creator what needs to be done

[9]

Answers

Topic 1 — The Media Industry

Pages 4-5: Sectors

1   E.g. A group of organisations that make products in the media sector. *[1 mark]*
    Sectors exist in the traditional and new media areas.

2   film *[1 mark]*

3   Any one from: radio / television / print publishing *[1 mark]*

4   They existed before the development of computers and the internet. *[1 mark]*

5   A newspaper is a media product produced by the print **publishing** sector. *[1 mark]*

6   Any two from: e.g. online distribution / streaming / promoting on social media / development of VFX/SFX / increase in resolution/frame rate. *[2 marks available — 1 mark for each]*

7   Systems that require user input and respond to choices and actions are produced by the **interactive** media sector. *[1 mark]*

8   computer games *[1 mark]*

9   Any two from: e.g. social media platforms / streaming services / messaging services *[2 marks available — 1 mark for each]*

10 digital publishing *[1 mark]*

11 Any two from: e.g. streaming / VR / AR / smartphones / AI / CGI *[2 marks available — 1 mark for each]*

Page 6: Products

1   photographer *[1 mark]*

2   Any two from: e.g. digital imaging and graphics / comics and graphic novels / eBooks *[2 marks available — 1 mark for each]*

3
Media sector	Tick if the media sector uses digital games	Tick if the media sector uses websites
internet	✓	✓
print publishing		✓
interactive media	✓	✓

[2 marks available — 1 mark for each correct row]

4   E.g. audio / music *[2 marks available — 1 mark for each]*

5   AR stands for **augmented reality** and VR stands for **virtual reality**. *[2 marks available — 1 mark for each]*

Pages 7-8: Job Roles in the Media Industry

1
Type of role	Creative roles	Technical roles	Senior roles
Job	copy writer	video editor	campaign manager
	script writer	camera operator	director

[2 marks available — 1 mark for each]

2   animator *[1 mark]*
    Production manager is a senior role. Audio technician and web developer are technical roles.

3   production *[1 mark]*

4   A web **designer** is responsible for the overall look of web pages and website across multiple platforms. A web **developer** builds websites, uploads content and maintains working websites. *[2 marks available — 1 mark for each]*

5   Any one from: e.g. video / audio / animation / digital games *[1 mark]*

6   The **director** will manage the positioning of cameras and actors on a film set. *[1 mark]*

7   Any two from: e.g. sound editor / video editor / web developer *[2 marks available — 1 mark for each]*

8   production manager *[1 mark]*

9   Any two from: e.g. animator / content creator / graphic designer / illustrator / graphic artist / photographer *[2 marks available — 1 mark for each]*

10 Any one from: e.g. managing the creation of promotional material / managing the marketing campaign *[1 mark]*

11 Any two from: e.g. game programmer / game developer / web developer / web designer *[2 marks available — 1 mark for each]*

Topic 2 — Factors Influencing Product Design

Page 9: Purpose, Language and Tone

1   Collect data *[1 mark]*

2   E.g. (to) educate *[1 mark]*

3   E.g. the feeling or mood created by the words used *[1 mark]*

4   A newsreader would use **formal** language whereas an influencer would use **informal** language. *[2 marks available — 1 mark for each]*

5   E.g. friendly / fun / simple *[1 mark]*

6   Any two from: e.g. video (such as TV) / audio (such as radio) / digital imaging and graphics (such as posters) / social media platforms or apps *[2 marks available — 1 mark for each]*

Page 10: Style, Content and Layout

1   E.g. the category or style of a media product *[1 mark]*

2   E.g. the positioning of elements on a product *[1 mark]*

3   Any two from: e.g. complex scientific words / made-up words / advanced technology / space travel / time travel / robots / aliens *[2 marks available — 1 mark for each convention]*

4   Any two from: e.g. voice recordings / music / sound effects *[2 marks available — 1 mark for each]*

5   Black and white colour scheme *[1 mark]*

Page 11: Audience

1   Any two from: e.g. age / gender / occupation / income / education / location / interests / lifestyle *[2 marks available — 1 mark for each]*

2   Income *[1 mark]*

3
Category	Description of the category	Example of how an audience characteristic could influence product design
Location	Where a person lives	People living in the countryside may be more attracted to products that focus on the natural environment
Age	How old someone is	E.g. young children will be attracted to bright colours.

[2 marks available — 1 mark for each correct answer]

4   Any one from: e.g. it allows market research to be more effective / it allows products to be designed to appeal to a specific audience / it allows opportunities for new products to be identified *[1 mark]*

Page 12: Client Requirements

1   Primary research methods *[1 mark]*

2   E.g. how much time is available for completing a task/set of tasks/project *[1 mark]*

3   purpose *[1 mark]*

4   The final product must align with the overall ethos and **branding** of the client organisation. An organisation's ethos is its **values** and the things it cares about. *[2 marks available — 1 mark for each]*

Answers

5   Any two from: e.g. content / genre / style / theme
   [2 marks available — 1 mark for each]

6   E.g. an organisation's rules around logos, colours, fonts and images
   [1 mark]

Page 13: Client Brief Formats

1   E.g. A client brief sets out the requirements that a new product must meet. *[1 mark]*

2   A risk assessment *[1 mark]*

3   Any one from: e.g. formal briefs typically include clear descriptions whereas informal briefs may not / informal briefs are normally created between clients and designers who know each other well whereas for a formal brief there might not be an existing relationship / formal briefs usually involve written documentation and meetings whereas an informal brief may just be an informal conversation, text or email *[1 mark]*

4   Any one from: e.g. commission / written *[1 mark]*

5   Any two from: e.g. scope of the product / costs / timescales / reuse of existing products
   [2 marks available — 1 mark for each]

Page 14: Research Data and Methods

1   Questionnaires *[1 mark]*

2   Any two from: e.g. it is instantly available / it is easy to access / it can be cheap or free to access / it exists for a wide range of topics and genres / you can benefit from information written by experts *[2 marks available — 1 mark for each advantage]*

3   Any two from: e.g. it could be inaccurate/biased / it might be out of date / information you need might not be available / you can't ask follow-up questions
   [2 marks available — 1 mark for each disadvantage]

4   Any one from: e.g. polls / surveys / questionnaires *[1 mark]*

5   E.g. data that is given in words, which could include opinions, reasons or explanations *[1 mark]*
   Quantitative data is about quantities (numbers). If you remember this, you know that qualitative data is the other one.

6   Any one advantage from: e.g. cheap to access / easy to access / presenters/contributors can be specialists
   Any one disadvantage from: e.g. some programmes may be biased / information presented may be inaccurate/poorly researched
   [2 marks available — 1 mark for each]

Page 15: Media Codes

1   Any one from: e.g. To suggest meaning to an audience / To create an impact / To engage an audience *[1 mark]*

2   The angle of a camera. *[1 mark]*

3   **Symbolic** codes often involve colours. For example, the colour green often conveys something about **nature**.
   [2 marks available — 1 mark for each]

4   Any two from: e.g. typography / positioning / language
   [2 marks available — 1 mark for each]

5   Any one from: e.g. sound effects / music / voice recording *[1 mark]*

Page 16: Colour, Graphics and Typography

1   (a) What letters look like is called **typography**. *[1 mark]*
    (b) Option B / the middle example *[1 mark]*

2   (a) E.g. The shape/triangles are associated with warning signs. *[1 mark]*
    (b) Any two from: e.g. they contrast with each other / they are associated with danger / they are often used for warning signs
       [2 marks available — 1 mark for each]

3   Serif *[1 mark]*

Page 17: Lighting, Movement and Mise-en-scène

1   E.g. video / special effects / digital imaging and graphics / digital games *[1 mark]*

2   Mise-en-scène *[1 mark]*

3   Characters involved in a car chase *[1 mark]*

4   Mise-en-scène includes things such as the actors, **costume** design, set and **lighting**. *[2 marks available — 1 mark for each]*

5   E.g. The position of actors in a frame. *[1 mark]*

6   Any two from: e.g. high-key / low-key / underlighting / warm / cool / three-point
   [2 marks available — 1 mark for each type of lighting]

Page 18: Camera Techniques and Transitions

1   How the director frames an actor depends on the type of shot and the **angle** of the camera. *[1 mark]*

2   Close up *[1 mark]*

3   E.g. a high angle / a long/wide shot / an overhead/aerial shot *[1 mark]*

4

Technique	Example	Possible reason for use
Over the shoulder		So the viewer feels they are part of the conversation
Ground level		E.g. to make the viewer seem smaller / to make the character seem larger / to introduce a new character dramatically.
Aerial/overhead/drone		Viewers can see the layout and size of the scene, and how the characters interact

   [2 marks available — 1 mark for each correct answer]

5   E.g. zoom / track / tilt / pan *[1 mark]*

Page 19: Audio

1   E.g. fade / a sudden start/stop *[1 mark]*
   If you put 'fade in' or 'fade out' that's also correct.

2   Vocal intonation *[1 mark]*

3   Audio added to a product in post-production includes music and **sound** effects. *[1 mark]*

4   E.g. to increase the tension/suspense of a scene / to make the audience think / to show how quiet the environment is / to give a feeling of awkwardness *[1 mark]*

5   (a) Any one from: e.g. dialogue / speech / words to be spoken *[1 mark]*
    (b) Foley artist *[1 mark]*

Page 20: Animations and Interactivity

1   Any two from: e.g. social media platforms / apps / digital games / websites / multimedia
   [2 marks available — 1 mark for each product]

2   When a product responds to the actions of a user in some way this is called **interactivity**. *[1 mark]*
   If you gave 'interactive' as the missing word this is also worth 1 mark.

3   E.g. What the user sees changes when the user turns their head. *[1 mark]*

4   E.g. a user can see computer-generated images in their environment through their smartphone camera. *[1 mark]*

5   Any two from: e.g. parts can change when you hover the cursor over them / animations can be used to show a page is loading / menus can pop-down/pop-out for navigation / image galleries can scroll through images / animated objects/characters can be used
   [2 marks available — 1 mark for each]

6   A clip of a reporter giving a live news report on TV. *[1 mark]*

Answers

Topic 3 — Pre-production Planning

Page 21: Work Planning

1 contingencies *[1 mark]*
2 workflow *[1 mark]*
3 Any two from: e.g. production phases / tasks / activities / timescales / milestones *[2 marks available — 1 mark for each]*
4 Any two from: e.g. people / equipment / software *[2 marks available — 1 for each]*
5 A = task *[1 mark]*, B = pre-production *[1 mark]*

Page 22: Mind Maps and Mood Boards

1 E.g. To quickly generate ideas. *[1 mark]*
2 A mind map usually starts with a key idea called the **node**. This is then broken down into **sub-nodes**. *[2 marks available — 1 for each]*
3 Any one from: e.g. presentation software / Microsoft® PowerPoint® / Keynote / Canva® *[1 mark]*
4 colour schemes *[1 mark]*
5 Any one from: e.g. graphic designer / creative director / web designer / client *[1 mark]*
   There are lots of users you could put here.
6 Any one from: e.g. sounds / videos / animations / hyperlinks *[1 mark]*

Page 23: Planning Documents

1 Any two from: e.g. asset name / reference number / file name / properties / source / copyright / description of how it's used in project *[2 marks available — 1 mark for each]*
2 Any two from: e.g. images / sounds / videos / logos / shapes *[2 marks available — 1 mark for each]*
3 E.g. flowchart *[1 mark]*
   Any interactive product that has links between pages or sections is likely to be planned using a flowchart.
4 processes *[1 mark]*
   Each step in a process is shown in a specific shape. Arrows are then used to show the flow from one step to another in the correct order.
5 ◇ — a decision *[1 mark]*
   ▭ — an action/process *[1 mark]*

Page 24: Storyboards and Scripts

1 events in a film *[1 mark]*
2 Any two from: e.g. director / animator / graphic designer / editor / video editor *[2 marks available — 1 mark for each]*
3 Any two from: e.g. video / animation / digital games / comics and graphic novels *[2 marks available — 1 mark for each]*
4 Any two from: e.g. actors / directors / camera operators / editors *[2 marks available — 1 mark for each]*
5 Any one from: e.g. audio / animation *[1 mark]*
6 E.g. the dialogue to be spoken by the characters/actors *[1 mark]*

Page 25: Visualisation Diagrams and Wireframes

1 a film poster *[1 mark]*
2 Any two from: e.g. digital artwork / concept sketches / placeholder text / annotations / questions for the client to consider *[2 marks available — 1 mark for each]*
   Annotations can be about things like fonts, colours, sizes and styles so you can still get a mark if you used one of those in your answer.
3 Any two from: e.g. graphic designers / clients / animators / web designers / copy writers / content creators *[2 marks available — 1 mark for each]*
4 E.g. app / website *[1 mark]*

5

Block	What it typically represents
▤	A piece of text
⊠	An image

[2 marks available — 1 mark for each]

Page 26: Protecting the Individual

1 Permission is not needed before filming in a **public** place. *[1 mark]*
2 the owner *[1 mark]*
3 E.g. get their permission *[1 mark]*
4 Taking photos of someone through the window of their home without their permission is an invasion of **privacy** *[1 mark]*
5 libel *[1 mark]*
6 slander *[1 mark]*
7 Organisations must keep personal data in case it is useful for something in the future. *[1 mark]*

Page 27: Intellectual Property

1 Any two from: e.g. writing / illustration / photography / film / music recordings *[2 marks available — 1 mark for each]*
   Anything that has been created by an individual is automatically protected by copyright.
2 patents *[1 mark]*
3 Any two from: e.g. a design / artwork / phrase / sound / logo / colour *[2 marks available — 1 mark for each]*
4 Creative Commons / CC *[1 mark]*
5 Using copyrighted work without permission for research or personal study is known as fair **dealing**. *[1 mark]*
6 password *[1 mark]*
7 E.g. taken to court / fine / prison sentence *[1 mark]*
   The consequences vary depending on the seriousness of the offence.

Page 28: Health and Safety

1 E.g. What should be done to mitigate each risk / who might be harmed by each risk / who is responsible for mitigating each risk *[1 mark]*
2 Any two from: e.g. using computers / long working hours / being in unfamiliar environments for a location recce *[2 marks — 1 mark for each]*
3 Any two from: e.g. moving heavy equipment / electric shocks from exposed wires / exposure to chemicals / explosives *[2 marks available — 1 mark for each]*
   Making a film can be risky, even if you aren't a stunt person. There are loads of possible hazards you could list here.
4 Any two from: e.g. restrict access to only people working on the production / allow people regular breaks / carry out regular equipment checks / use virtual sets *[2 marks available — 1 mark for each]*
5 A visit to a possible filming location before filming begins is known as a location **recce**. *[1 mark]*
6 E.g. to check the suitability for filming *[1 mark]*

Page 29: Regulation, Certification and Classification

1 Advertising Standards Authority *[1 mark]*
2 Any two from: e.g. because it is misleading / because it is offensive / because it is irresponsible / because it is harmful *[1 mark]*
3 newspapers *[1 mark]*
4 BBFC / British Board of Film Classification *[1 mark]*
5 Any one from: e.g. swearing / drugs / violence / dangerous behaviour / sex / horror / discrimination *[1 mark]*
6 computer/video games *[1 mark]*
7 Europe *[1 mark]*

Answers

Topic 4 — Distribution Considerations

Page 30: Distribution Platforms

1 Interactive TV *[1 mark]*
CDs/DVDs are examples of physical media but aren't physical platforms.

2 (a) kiosk *[1 mark]*

(b) Any one from: e.g. Easier for customers to use / Quicker for the staff / Don't need a staff member to take the orders / Customers can place their order in a language they understand / Orders will be accurately recorded *[1 mark]*

3 E.g. websites *[1 mark]*
apps *[1 mark]*

4 Any one from: e.g. Users can access content at any time and from anywhere / Content can be distributed around the world to a larger market / Media products can be easily updated / Removes the need for transporting physical materials and so is cheaper *[1 mark]*

Page 31: Distribution Media

1 Media can be distributed using **physical** products such as CDs and DVDs. *[1 mark]*
CDs and DVDs are just two examples of types of physical media that can be used to store and distribute content.

2 (a) Any one from: e.g. They are cheap to produce / Customers are familiar with using DVDs / They have enough capacity to hold a full length film / They are portable *[1 mark]*

(b) Any one from: e.g. The customer needs a DVD player/drive (many modern computers do not have them) / They are easily damaged / They take time to ship to customers *[1 mark]*

3 (a) USB/memory stick *[1 mark]*

(b) Any one from: e.g. Memory sticks may not be compatible with all operating systems / Many devices no longer have a standard USB port that allows the memory stick to be connected *[1 mark]*

4 Any two from: e.g. book / magazine / newspaper / photograph *[2 marks available — 1 mark for each]*

Page 32: File Compression

1 One reason that files get compressed is to reduce the file **size**. Another reason is to reduce the time it takes to **upload** the files to an online platform. *[2 marks available — 1 mark for each]*

2 Compression that permanently deletes part of a file is called **lossy** compression *[1 mark]*

3 lossy *[1 mark]*

4 E.g. Sending a high-resolution print file by email *[1 mark]*

5 It's often used when archiving files *[1 mark]*
It's important to keep the original data when archiving files so lossless compression is used for this.

Page 33: Image Files

1 A **vector** image uses coordinates, colours and curves to represent the shapes. A **bitmap** image is made up of a grid of pixels.
[2 marks available — 1 mark for each]

2 a photo of a landscape *[1 mark]*

3 E.g. The quality of the image will increase *[1 mark]*.
The file size will increase *[1 mark]*.

4
File format	Vector or bitmap?
.tiff	bitmap
.jpg	bitmap
.svg	vector

[2 marks available — 1 mark for each correct answer]

5 An image is 4000 pixels wide and 2000 pixels tall. This is called its pixel **dimension**. *[1 mark]*

Page 34: Audio Files

1 E.g. sample rate *[1 mark]*
bit depth *[1 mark]*

2 bits *[1 mark]*

3 Sample rate is the number of samples taken each **second**. *[1 mark]*

4 E.g. lower sound quality *[1 mark]*
smaller file size *[1 mark]*

5 Any one from: e.g. online transfer / streaming *[1 mark]*

6 lossy *[1 mark]*

7 E.g. .wav *[1 mark]*

Page 35: Moving Image Files

1 Any one from: e.g. video / animation *[1 mark]*

2 HD *[1 mark]*

3 definition *[1 mark]*

4 The resolution of a moving image file relates to the number of **pixels** in each **frame**. *[2 marks available — 1 mark for each]*

5 Any two from: e.g. .avi / .mov / .mp4 / .gif
[2 marks available — 1 mark for each]

6 A disadvantage of using a higher frame rate is a larger **file size**. *[1 mark]*

Mixed Practice

Page 36-38: Mixed Practice

1 (a) influence *[1 mark]*
It's trying to get you to do something, but isn't educating you or informing you about why you should do it.

(b) symbolic *[1 mark]*

(c) Any one from: e.g. graphic designer / copy writer / illustrator / graphic artist *[1 mark]*

(d) Any two from: e.g. visualisation diagram / concept sketch / asset log / mood board / mind map
[2 marks available — 1 mark for each]

2 audio *[1 mark]*

3 Any two from: e.g. files load faster on websites / the smaller files upload more quickly to streaming platforms / the smaller files transfer more quickly online / file size is smaller
[2 marks available — 1 mark for each]

4 digital images *[1 mark]*

5 advertising *[1 mark]*

6 establishing shot *[1 mark]*

7 negotiated *[1 mark]*

8 Any two from: e.g. they can be damaged easily / they can create waste / they are expensive to distribute
[2 marks available — 1 mark for each]

9 risk assessment *[1 mark]*

10 genre *[1 mark]*

11 milestones *[1 mark]*

Section B — Scenario 1

Pages 44-51: Nostalgic Flicks

1 People aged 8-13 years / People interested in watching the films shown by Nostalgic Flicks / People living near to the cinema *[1 mark]*

2 (a) BBFC / British Board of Film Classification *[1 mark]*

(b) E.g. Films are given age certificates. The age certificates give guidance about the ages or minimum age that a film is suitable for. *[2 marks available — 1 mark for identifying a classification and 1 mark for describing it]*

Answers

3   Any three from:
E.g. A director must communicate with the client (Nostalgic Flicks) / they must manage the cast and crew on set / they would work with other senior roles (e.g. a creative director) / they would manage the filming (e.g. deciding on the camera angles) / they would work with an editor in post-production
[3 marks available — 1 mark for each valid responsibility]

4   (a) secondary research *[1 mark]*
     (b) E.g. The manager is finding/using information collected by someone else. *[1 mark]*

5   (a) qualitative (data) *[1 mark]*
     (b) You may have identified any of these research methods:
     Focus groups / interviews / surveys / questionnaires
     E.g. The manager could have conducted focus groups with people who were children in the 1980s or 1990s to ask them which films they watched and enjoyed.
     [2 marks available — 1 mark for identifying a primary research method and 1 mark for describing how the manager would use it]

6   quantitative (data) *[1 mark]*

7   You may have included the following strengths, weaknesses and improvements in your answer:

Strengths
E.g. The images used are relevant to what is being advertised. They show a cinema audience and a boy who seems to be of an age within the target audience mentioned.
The text all looks large enough to be read clearly, so the details are easy to read for the person reading the advertisement.
Important details are given that make it clear that the cinema is promoting a summer film programme for children ages 8-13.
The colours offer high contrast (e.g. white text against a dark blue background) so the text can be easily read.

Weaknesses
E.g. Some important information is missing (e.g. where to find the cinema or what films are showing). This means that people reading the advert don't have all the information they need to decide if they can/will attend.
Some of the wording in the advertisement is targeted at children (e.g. are you between 8 and 13?) so it's not suitable for use in a magazine aimed at adults. Using wording aimed towards parents/ guardians is more suitable in the lifestyle magazine.
The text in the speech bubble doesn't sound like the voice of a young boy as the photo suggests. This does not seem appropriate for the target audience.
The audience in the image does not appear to contain many children, which is strange considering that the advertisement is targeting children.

Improvements
E.g. Add in extra details such as where the cinema is located and some example films that are being shown.
Add something to indicate where to go for more information, e.g. a link to a website or a QR code.
Make the wording on the whole advertisement so it's targeted either at children or at parents/guardians.
Change the text in the speech bubble so it sounds like a child speaking or change the photo so it's an adult.
Change the audience photo to one that shows some children.
Your answer doesn't need to be split out into three parts like this. It's just done this way here so you can see the different points that could make up your answer.

How to grade your answer:

7-9 marks: The answer is thorough and shows detailed understanding. A variety of strengths and weaknesses are discussed. The answer clearly considers how suitable the advertisement is for its purpose and target audience, suggests a range of improvements and regularly uses appropriate terminology.

4-6 marks: The answer is adequate and shows sound understanding. Some strengths and/or weaknesses are discussed. The answer attempts to consider how suitable the advertisement is for its purpose and target audience, suggests some improvements and sometimes uses appropriate terminology.

1-3 marks: The answer is brief and shows limited understanding. Few strengths or weaknesses are discussed. The answer makes only a limited attempt to consider how suitable the advertisement is for its purpose and target audience, suggests few improvements and uses minimal appropriate terminology.

0 marks: There is no relevant information.

8   (a) Any three from: tasks / activities / workflow / timescales
     [3 marks available — 1 mark for each component identified]
     (b) Any one from: phases / milestones / contingencies / resources
     [1 mark]
     (c) You may have included two of the following points in your answer:
     E.g. Workplans can make it clear what tasks need to be done so there is less risk of something important being forgotten.
     Workplans can show deadlines for the tasks so there is less risk of the project overrunning as everyone is aware when each task needs to be completed.
     Workplans can allocate work to each staff member so there is less confusion about what each person is responsible for.
     [4 marks available — 1 mark for each advantage up to a maximum of two advantages and 1 mark for each explanation]

9   (a) E.g. Compression reduces file size, which means it takes less time to upload.
     [2 marks available — 1 mark for identifying a benefit and 1 mark for explaining the benefit]
     Don't just say 'size' on its own — you need to be more specific to get the marks. For example, here it's better to say 'file size'.
     (b) lossy compression *[1 mark]*
     Lossy compression is more effective at reducing file size than lossless for images, audio and video. Lossy should be used as quality is less important when uploading content to social media.
     (c) You may have included the following reasons in your answer:
     E.g. The cinema will not want to use lossy compression because it will cause a reduction in quality that is likely to be noticed on the large screen.
     The films might be held on film rather than digitally because of their age, which means they cannot be compressed.
     [2 marks available — 1 mark for giving a reason and 1 mark for explaining it]
     This question requires you to think about the scenario. Cinemas have large screens so any loss of quality might be noticed. The films being shown could be quite old so might be stored on film. This means you can't compress them in the same way you can with more recent films that are stored as digital files.

10   E.g. The films shown are all from before 2000, which is before videos (including films) were commonly available in resolutions higher than SD (such as HD, 4K or UHD).
     [2 marks available — 1 mark for stating the reason and 1 mark for explaining it]

11   (a) Any one from: e.g. graphic designer / illustrator / graphic artist / content creator / copy writer / campaign manager *[1 mark]*
     (b) Your answer may include any one of the following points:
     E.g. It should be bright and colourful so that it attracts the attention of children aged 8-13 / It could have the names of all the films the cinema is showing so that it's clear what will be shown / It should use informal language that appeals more to children
     [2 marks available — 1 mark for identifying an element of the poster and 1 mark for an explanation]

Answers

12 Your storyboard may include reference to the following features, how they are used and how their use has been improved:

Sketches for each scene and detail about what happens

E.g. The sketch for each scene can be rough but it should clearly show what is happening.

In fig. 3 one scene doesn't have a sketch so the director doesn't know how it should look. In your improved storyboard you should ensure every scene has a sketch.

Also in fig. 3 the clapperboard scene doesn't have any detail about what information should be shown. You could add some details within the picture or in the description below.

Relevance of the content

E.g. The scenes should be relevant to the summer film programme, so at least some scenes should be based in a cinema.

The scenes in fig. 3 are all relevant but an 'older teenager' has been mentioned in the storyboard which doesn't fit with the target audience for the campaign. To improve this you could include a child in the target audience instead (perhaps with a parent/guardian too).

The order of scenes should be clear

E.g. Your storyboard should match the convention of being read left to right and each scene should be numbered to make the order clear.

In fig. 3 it's not clear which order the scenes are in and the numbering does not look correct.

Timing information

E.g. It is useful for a director to see information about how long a scene should be. This can be added into the description. Adding this would be an improvement from fig. 3 where there is no timing information given.

Other information needed for the director or video editor

E.g. This includes the type of shot required (e.g. a low angle shot) and the scene transitions. In your improved storyboard these could be added to the description of each scene.

How to grade your answer:

7-9 marks:	The storyboard is comprehensive and shows detailed understanding. A range of suggested improvements are discussed which cover a variety of components and conventions. The answer clearly considers how suitable the storyboard is for the client's requirements.
4-6 marks:	The storyboard is adequate and shows sound understanding. Some suggested improvements are discussed which cover some components and conventions. The answer makes some attempt to consider how suitable the storyboard is for the client's requirements.
1-3 marks:	The storyboard is basic and shows limited understanding. Few suggested improvements are discussed which cover few components and conventions. The answer makes only a limited attempt to consider how suitable the storyboard is for the client's requirements.
0 marks:	There is no relevant information.

13 (a) Any two from: television / radio / print publishing
[2 marks available — 1 mark for each]

(b) You may have included two of the following points in your answer:
E.g. Some films are released directly to online streaming platforms. This means the film industry is moving away from the tradition of releasing all films in cinemas before they become available on other platforms.
Instead of physical media like DVDs, many films are only distributed online through streaming platforms. This means that films are now more accessible to more people as you no longer need specialised hardware (e.g. DVD players) to watch them.

Films are often promoted on social media or on platforms like YouTube™. This has changed how films get promoted to the general public, e.g. short clips of actors talking about their film gets posted on social media rather than adverts in more traditional media.
Advancements in CGI and special effects in general have allowed films to create increasingly impressive and realistic visuals. This means that there are more jobs for people in the film industry who create special effects.
[4 marks available — 1 mark for each way digital technology has evolved and 1 mark for each description]

14 (a) An example answer would be:
E.g. Special effects are visual tricks that are often used to create scenes that are difficult to do in real life. For example, special effects could be used to blow up a car in an action film scene.
[2 marks available — 1 mark for describing what special effects are and 1 mark for giving an example]

(b) E.g. Visual effects are special effects added in post-production editing. For example, they can be used to insert a computer-generated dragon into a scene.
[2 marks available — 1 mark for describing what VFX are and 1 mark for giving an example]

15 (a) Your answer may include any one of the following points:
E.g. To keep an up-to-date record of what assets (e.g. images) are used on the project / to keep a record of the properties of each asset. *[1 mark]*

(b) You may have included the following points in your answer:
E.g. Copyright protects your intellectual property, such as photographs, automatically and you don't have to apply for it. The © symbol can be used to show when something is protected by copyright but work is still protected even if the symbol isn't shown.
Copyright protection means that the photos can't be used without the permission of the person who owns them.
[2 marks available — 1 mark for each point]
It's not relevant to talk about patents or trademarks in your answer because these aren't used for photographs.

(c) You may have included some of the following points in your answer:
E.g. The graphic designer could come up with ideas for visual content. The ideas can be discussed with other colleagues and developed further by creating mind maps and mood boards.
The graphic designer could create planning documents such as an asset log. The asset log would mean that an accurate record of asset properties would be kept.
The graphic designer could export images and graphics for the advert in a suitable format for the magazine. This would mean that the images and graphics in the advert would print clearly in the magazine.

How to grade your answer:

5-6 marks:	The explanation is thorough and shows detailed understanding. Two responsibilities are identified and explained. The answer shows detailed understanding of the role's responsibilities, clearly explains their contribution and regularly uses appropriate terminology.
3-4 marks:	The explanation is adequate and shows sound understanding. Two responsibilities are identified and at least one of them is explained. The answer shows some understanding of the role's responsibilities, adequately explains their contribution and uses some appropriate terminology.

Answers

1-2 marks   The explanation is brief and shows limited understanding. At least one responsibility is identified and at least one is partially explained. The answer shows limited understanding of the role's responsibilities, explains their contribution in a basic way and uses minimal appropriate terminology.

0 marks: There is no relevant information.

Section B — Scenario 2

Pages 52-59: Rooftop Rangers

1 (a) Any two from: e.g. (to) advertise / educate / inform / influence
      [2 marks available — 1 mark for each valid purpose]

  (b) (i) E.g. Audience segmentation splits an audience into different categories. *[1 mark]*
     (ii) Any one from: e.g. age / gender / occupation / income / education / location / interests / lifestyle *[1 mark]*

  (c) You may have included the following points in your answer:
Segmentation can be used help identify a specific audience so that products can be designed which best meet the needs of that audience. This means the product is more likely to sell well.

It allows market research and marketing to be more effective. This is because it can be specifically focused on the target audience.

It allows opportunities for new products to be worked out. This can be done by working out which audience segments aren't having their needs met by existing products.
      [4 marks available — 1 mark for each benefit up to a maximum of 2 marks and 1 mark for each linked explanation]

2 (a) The most appropriate hardware devices include: e.g. computer / laptop / tablet
The most appropriate software includes: e.g. image editing software / presentation software / word processors
      [2 marks available — 1 mark for identifying a hardware device and 1 mark for identifying a type of software]

  (b) Your mood board may include reference to the following:

A number of pieces of content from Fig. 1

Your new mood board should have around 6-8 pieces of content. Using this number of pieces will give a good number of different ideas to consider and be inspired by.

It's important not to repeat any pieces more than once. In Fig. 2 two pieces of content are repeated (the photo of a trainer). This isn't necessary and takes up valuable space. If the two trainers are supposed to show different ideas, they need to be more clearly different or annotated.

Relevant pieces of content from Fig. 1

In your new mood board you could have used, for example, pieces 1, 2, 3, 5, 7, 9, 12 and 13 to give a good variety of relevant content.

These pieces of content are relevant for a variety of reasons. Although you do not need to provide detailed reasons in your mood board, the annotations you write should explain why a piece of content is relevant. E.g. The photo of concrete (3) is relevant because parkour typically takes place in urban environments where there's concrete. The photo of the young woman jumping over a wall (5) is relevant as it shows someone perhaps doing some parkour.

Some of the pieces of content, such as numbers 4, 6, 15 and 16 are not really relevant so should not be included. The photo of rugby players (4) and the photo of grass (6) seem unlikely to be useful inspiration for on the mood board.

Layout of the mood board

Mood boards tend to be larger than Fig. 2 and on the page you have more space to design your mood board.

Arranging the content in your mood board horizontally (as seen in Fig. 2) might make it harder to group the pieces of content together into different areas (for example, cartoon artwork together or content containing audio) and also to see possible links between them.

The range of content used

Fig. 2 only uses a limited range of different content (photos, cartoons and logos) but an improved mood board would also include other types of content such as text.

This limited range of content might limit the ideas that can be generated from the mood board.

To increase the range of content, some additional ideas could go on the mood board. For example, additional colours and shapes for the group's crest could be added.

How to grade your answer:

7-9 marks: The mood board is comprehensive and shows detailed understanding. A range of suggested improvements are identified which cover a variety of components. The answer clearly considers how suitable the mood board is for the client's new logo.

4-6 marks: The mood board is adequate and shows sound understanding. Some suggested improvements are identified which cover some components. The answer makes some attempt to consider how suitable the mood board is for the client's new logo.

1-3 marks: The mood board is basic and shows limited understanding. Few suggested improvements are identified which cover few components. The answer makes only a limited attempt to consider how suitable the mood board is for the client's new logo.

0 marks: There is no relevant information.

3 **Advantages**:
E.g. Magazines and newspapers can be reliable sources. This means they can be trusted to contain correct information.
They are often cheaper to buy compared to other methods. This makes newspapers and magazines a more accessible research source than others, e.g. books and journals.
They are published regularly. This means they can contain up-to-date information.
Some magazines and newspapers contain specialised information as they focus on a particular topic. This might not be available from other research sources.

Disadvantages:
E.g. Some magazines and newspapers are opinion-based. This means the information could be biased.
Free alternatives are available online whereas magazines and newspapers usually have to be paid for. This means they can be an expensive option.
The information you need might not be in the latest issue of the newspaper/magazine. This means the information might be out-of-date.
[4 marks available — 1 mark for identifying an advantage, 1 mark for identifying a disadvantage and 1 mark for each linked description]

4 You may have included two of the following points in your answer:
E.g. The text on the left is bold, but the text on the right is not.
The text on the left is underlined, but the text on the right is not.
The text on the left is in a sans serif font, whereas the text on the right is in a serif font.
[2 marks available — 1 mark for each valid difference]
Typography is just a fancy word for how the text looks.

Answers

75

5 (a) (i) dots per inch *[1 mark]*
(ii) pixels per inch *[1 mark]*
(b) Any one of: e.g. Vector image files do not represent complex images well since they only represent an image with basic shapes / They can't be used for photos since photos are too complicated to represent with basic shapes / They are not as widely compatible as bitmaps since they need specialist vector image software to edit.
[2 marks available — 1 mark for identifying a disadvantage and 1 mark for explaining it]

6 You may have included the following strengths, weaknesses and improvements in your answer:
Strengths
E.g. The main components of the logo are clear (the two letters, rectangular shape and graphic). This clearly shows what needs to be included in the logo.
There are two annotations, although one is crossed out. This shows the graphic designer that the stick person will need to be changed to match the description.
Some shading is used to indicate colour. This helps the graphic designer to know to add colours or patterns to the letters and the rectangle.
Weaknesses
E.g. Only one annotation is used so the graphic designer might be unsure about certain aspects of the design.
Some parts could be incomplete. The second letter 'R' has some lines inside and the designer might not know whether or not this is deliberate from this diagram alone.
A lack of neatness makes it hard for the graphic designer to know the exact style that is wanted. It is not clear what the rectangular shape at the bottom of the logo is meant to represent.
The stick person is very basic and does not show a person doing parkour. The graphic designer might not know what Rooftop Rangers want here.
Improvements
E.g. Add more annotations to assist the designer. For example, more information about things like colour and font. This will improve the visualisation diagram as the designer will know exactly what is wanted.
Change the parts of the diagram that look incomplete. If these are deliberate then add annotations to make it clear to the designer what is wanted. This will give the designer a better sense of the overall style of the logo.
Improve the parts of the diagram that aren't very neat and might be confusing for the designer. This would make it easier for the designer to see more clearly what each element is in the visualisation diagram.
Improve the stick figure in the diagram to give more information to the designers. For example, you could improve the stick figure to make it look like it was doing a parkour movement (or an add an annotation to explain this is what you want). This improvement would make it clear to the designer what the client wants the stick figure to look like in the final version.
How to grade your answer:
7-9 marks: The answer is thorough and shows detailed understanding. A variety of strengths and weaknesses are discussed. The answer clearly considers how suitable the diagram is for its purpose and target audience, suggests and explains a range of improvements and regularly uses appropriate terminology.
4-6 marks: The answer is adequate and shows sound understanding. Some strengths and/or weaknesses are discussed. The answer attempts to consider how suitable the diagram is for its purpose and target audience, suggests and explains some improvements and sometimes uses appropriate terminology.

1-3 marks: The answer is brief and shows limited understanding. Few strengths or weaknesses are discussed. The answer makes only a limited attempt to consider how suitable the diagram is for its purpose and target audience, suggests and explains few improvements and uses minimal appropriate terminology.
0 marks: There is no relevant information.
It's important to realise that this question is asking how suitable the visualisation diagram is for the graphic designer who actually has to make the logo, rather than whether or not the logo is suitable for the Rooftop Rangers.

7 E.g. A visit to a potential location to assess how suitable it is for filming. *[1 mark]*
A recce won't just look for hazards. It can also involve looking for the nearest shops, train stations or toilets too.

8 (a) Any three from: e.g. People may be injured whilst doing parkour / Stunts filmed at height may cause injuries due to falls / Weather such as rain or ice could make surfaces slippery and lead to injuries / Trailing wires can be a trip hazard / Electronic devices can overheat and cause fire / Chemicals used for special effects can cause injury if not handled properly / Food on set could cause an allergic reaction / Heavy equipment can fall and hurt people.
[3 marks available — 1 mark for each valid hazard]
You need to think about what can go wrong on a film set generally, but also specifically on this film set which involves people doing parkour on rooftops.

(b)

Hazard	E.g. People may be injured when doing parkour / Trailing wires can be a trip hazard / Food on set could cause an allergic reaction
Potential consequence	E.g. Bones could be broken from a hard landing / Someone could trip and hurt themselves / Someone with an allergy could have a reaction causing them to need to go to the hospital
Way to mitigate hazard	E.g. Place crash mats below any large jumps to reduce impact / Ensure camera operators tape down wires on set / Ensure that all people on set have their allergies recorded and the cooks are aware of this so they can change recipes if necessary

[2 marks available — 1 mark for a suitable potential consequence and 1 mark for a way to mitigate the hazard]
'Mitigate' means to make something less serious or reduce it.

9 You may have included the following points in your answer:
E.g. The angle of the camera can be used to make the viewer feel a certain way about the action. For example, a high angle shot could be used because it emphasises how high the actors are and makes the audience feel tense.
Different camera shots can be used to tell key parts of the story. For example, an extra wide shot could be used because it shows how far away the group are from the enemy.
The camera movement can be used to make the scene more exciting to watch. For example, tracking shots could be used to follow the actors as they run quickly because it makes the audience feel like they're running with them.
The lighting intensity/levels can be used to show what time of day the scene is taking place at. For example, an orange hue could be used to show the scene is taking place at sunset or sunrise.
The type of lighting used can frame certain actions. For example, strongly lighting the lead actor with a backlight could be used because it makes them stand out when they are on screen.
How to grade your answer:
5-6 marks: The explanation is thorough and shows detailed understanding. At least two techniques are identified and explained. The answer shows detailed understanding of both camera techniques and lighting and regularly uses appropriate terminology.

Answers

Answers

3-4 marks: The explanation is adequate and shows sound understanding. At least two techniques are identified and at least one of them is explained. The answer may only show some understanding of either camera techniques or lighting and uses some appropriate terminology.

1-2 marks: The explanation is brief and shows limited understanding. At least one technique is identified and at least one is partially explained. The answer uses minimal appropriate terminology.

0 marks: There is no relevant information.

10 (a) (i) E.g. Devices/items that are physical objects and are used to store and distribute content. *[1 mark]*

(ii) Any one from: e.g. CD / DVD / memory sticks / magazines / newspapers / books *[1 mark]*

(b) You may have included the following points in your answer:
E.g. Distributing online might give you access to a larger audience as the number of people watching films on physical media (such as DVDs) has fallen / The number of people that have access to devices that can play physical media, such as DVD players, is falling / Distributing online may create more exposure since popular film platforms have a wide audience / It may be cheaper than producing and shipping physical media such as DVDs.
[2 marks available — 1 mark for each valid reason]

11 You may have included one of the following points in your answer:
E.g. Their language should be slightly informal so that they come across as relatable, but still professional.
Their tone should be upbeat and friendly so viewers find the video enjoyable to watch.
They should use clear and concise language since the purpose of the video is to inform the audience about the filming process.
[2 marks available — 1 mark for identifying a possible adaptation to the tone of language and 1 mark for a linked explanation]

12 (a) You may have included two of the following points in your answer:
E.g. They are responsible for recording the video's audio. This needs to be consistently high quality.
They will set up microphones so that all cast members can be heard when they speak. This could involve clipping lapel mics to the members of the group or using a boom microphone above them.
They will monitor the audio while the interview is filmed so that they can quickly fix any issues that develop.
They might adjust the sound levels. For example, to minimise background noise.
[4 marks available — 1 mark for each responsibility up to a maximum of 2 marks and 1 mark for each linked point]

(b) You may have included two of the following points in your answer:
E.g. The camera could be in a fixed position because the people talking won't be moving around / The video might be filmed using an over the shoulder angle which is often used to show a conversation / The camera might be at eye level to help the members of the Rooftop Rangers connect more with the audience / The camera might pan from one person to another if the group are sitting together.
[4 marks available — 1 mark for each camera technique up to a maximum of 2 marks and 1 mark for each linked description]

Section B — Scenario 3

Pages 60-67: CPG Labs

1 Interactive media *[1 mark]*
Interactive media is anything where the user has lots of control over what it does, and it describes many apps and products that use AR.

2 (a) E.g. Augmented reality allows the user to experience the real world with some computer-generated images added. Virtual reality allows the user to experience a completely computer-generated world.
[2 marks available — 1 mark for describing AR and 1 mark for describing VR]

(b) Any from: e.g. video / multimedia / audio / music / animation / digital imaging and graphics *[1 mark]*

(c) Any two from: e.g. computers/laptops / interactive TVs / kiosks.
[2 marks available — 1 mark for each platform identified]

3 Any one from: e.g.
Some physical platforms have large screens (for example kiosks). This could mean that an image that looks fine on a smartphone could look blurry on a larger screen, so the pixel dimension may need to be increased. /
Some physical platforms have less storage capacity than others (for example, smartphones may have less storage than computers). This means that the pixel dimension should be as low as possible so unnecessary storage space isn't used up by having an image with larger dimensions than is required.
[2 marks available — 1 mark for a point and 1 mark for explaining it]
Increasing the pixel dimension means there are more pixels that need to be saved, so more storage space is required.

4 When considering to what extent the flow chart is fit for purpose you might have included the following strengths and weaknesses:
Strengths
E.g. Arrows are (generally) used to show the order in which different tasks take place. This could help the app creator know how to link tasks together.
A diamond shape has been used for a decision, with three clear outcomes. The app creator will know that they need to create/code three different outputs for this decision.
The shapes all have labels which describe what is needed. This leaves less decision-making for the app creator and allows them to focus on carrying out what the senior employee wants.
Weaknesses
E.g. There are two start shapes so the app creator might not be sure which one to begin with.
There is no option for the user to input which restaurant they are rating.
There is no end shape so the app creator might not be sure what ends this process, or the steps needed to get there.
Some arrows are missing and others are the wrong way round. This makes the order of the steps confusing and may lead to mistakes being made.
Rectangles are used to represent processes and inputs/outputs which isn't correct. It might help the app creator if the correct shapes for input/output were used (parallelograms).
Some processes are not covered in the flow chart. For example, the signing in process is not covered so the app creator will not know how this is supposed to work.
A decision is missing. The box 'Is the user signed in?' should be represented as a decision shape. This could mean that the app creator doesn't code this properly.
How to grade your answer:
7-9 marks: The answer is thorough and shows detailed understanding. The answer clearly considers how suitable the flow chart is for its purpose and target audience, suggests a range of improvements and regularly uses appropriate terminology. Suggested improvements are explained thoroughly.
4-6 marks: The answer is adequate and shows sound understanding. The answer attempts to consider how suitable the flow chart is for its purpose and target audience, suggests some improvements and sometimes uses appropriate terminology. Suggested improvements are explained adequately.

Answers

1-3 marks: The answer is brief and shows limited understanding. The answer makes only a limited attempt to consider how suitable the flow chart is for its purpose and target audience, suggests few improvements and uses minimal appropriate terminology. Suggested improvements are not explained clearly.

0 marks: There is no relevant information.

5 (a) E.g. A content creator produces digital content (e.g. a video or social media post) for a client. *[1 mark]*
   A common type of content creator is an 'influencer' who specifically makes content on social media for different clients. There are other content creators, but thinking about influencers may help remind you of what they do.

   (b) Any two from: e.g.
   Target audience – the client (CPG Labs) may have specified which target audience the video is being aimed at (e.g. young adults who eat out).
   Branding – the client may have provided branding to use in the video, such as the company/product logo, font and colours
   Content – the client may have provided text or specific images that need to appear in the video.
   Timescale – the client may have given a deadline based on when they wish to use the video to promote the product.
   Style – the client may have a house style that the video needs to follow, such as particular colours and logos, etc.
   [4 marks available — 1 mark for each requirement and 1 mark for each linked description]

   (c) Any two from: e.g. stage directions / character names / scene number / who is in a scene
   [2 marks available — 1 mark for each component identified]

   (d) Any two from: e.g.
   They might use different lighting techniques to ensure that the actors' faces are well-lit.
   They might use music to make the advert more engaging for viewers.
   They might use video editing software to add common effects like fading in and out of scenes, e.g. to suggest the passing of time.
   They might use close-up camera shots to focus the audience's attention on an actor's face and expressions.
   [2 marks available — 1 mark for identifying a technical code and 1 mark for describing how it could be used]

6 (a) (use/apply for a) trademark *[1 mark]*

   (b) E.g. They would need to contact the customers and get their permission to use the photos. This is necessary to make sure they're not breaking copyright law.
   [2 marks available — 1 mark for a point and 1 mark for explaining it]

   (c) You may have included the following points about collection, use and storage of personal data in your answer:
   Collection
   E.g. Customers have the right to be informed about what is being collected and why. This is so they can decide whether they are happy with it being collected or not. Only data the customers have consented to share should be collected, e.g. customers might agree for their email address to be collected but not their home address.
   Use
   E.g. The customers have the right to withdraw their consent at any time. This means the company has to stop using their data if they are asked to.
   It's a right of the customers that their data can only be used for things which they've given consent for. This means that CPG Labs can't change what they are using the data for without informing the customer.

Storage
E.g. Customers have the right to have their personal data securely stored. This means CPG Labs needs to make sure the data is kept safe and can't be accessed by anyone else.
Customers have the right to see what personal data is stored about them. This means that CPG Labs needs to send this personal data to customers if asked.
The customers have the right to update their personal data or ask to have it deleted. When asked, CPG Labs needs to change the data they have stored, or fully delete it.
How to grade your answer:

5-6 marks: The explanation is thorough and shows detailed understanding. A right is identified for all three areas and at least two are explained. The answer regularly uses appropriate terminology.

3-4 marks: The explanation is adequate and shows sound understanding. Two rights are identified that may fall under the same area and at least one of them is explained. The answer uses some appropriate terminology.

1-2 marks: The explanation is brief and shows limited understanding. At least one right is identified and partially explained. The answer uses minimal appropriate terminology.

0 marks: There is no relevant information.

7 (a) Any two from: e.g. animator / copy writer / script writer / content creator / graphic designer / illustrator/graphic artist / photographer / web designer.
   [2 marks available — 1 mark for each job role identified]

   (b) You need to give a description and phase of production for each job title you identified in part (a):
   E.g. An animator creates a sequence of images that create the illusion of movement. The majority of their work takes place in the production phase.
   A copy writer produces engaging written material and mainly works during the production phase.
   A script writer writes scripts and mainly works in the pre-production phase.
   A content creator produces original digital content and is mainly involved in production.
   A graphic designer produces visual content and mostly works during the production phase.
   An illustrator/graphic artist produces artwork and is mainly involved during production.
   A photographer uses a camera to produce high-quality images and does most of their work during production.
   A web designer designs web pages and is mainly involved in production.
   [4 marks available — 1 mark for describing each role's main responsibility and 1 mark for identifying the production phase]

   (c) You may have included the following points in your answer:
   E.g. Deciding on the creative vision and the visual identity of the company / working with others to create planning documents that clearly show how the creative vision should be applied / overseeing and conducting market research to see if the creative vision will be effective / leading the creative staff to ensure that the company's creative vision is implemented consistently / helping to manage projects to ensure that the creative work is completed on time and to a good standard / presenting the creative work to clients and other senior employees.
   [3 marks available — 1 mark for each responsibility described]

8 (a) ASA / Advertising Standards Authority *[1 mark]*

   (b) E.g. The ASA monitors all online or printed advertising in the UK to stop inappropriate content being seen by audiences. The ASA acts against adverts that are misleading, offensive, harmful or irresponsible.
   [2 marks available — 1 mark for each point about the role of the ASA]

(c) E.g. Defamation is when a false statement is made against a person or an organisation.
If CPG Labs use real reviews in the advert and they contain false or unfair content, the restaurant that has been reviewed could feel that they have been defamed.
[2 marks available — 1 mark for outlining what defamation is and 1 mark for outlining how it relates to the television advert]

(d) You may have included the following points in your answer:
E.g. Focus groups can be expensive to run because you need to pay the people taking part.
The focus group members can influence each other's views. This means that you might not get the real views of each individual in the group.
Focus groups can be difficult to arrange as it may be hard to find people willing to join the focus group.
It can take a long time to analyse results since qualitative information is not easily analysed by a computer.
The person leading the focus group could influence the group. This could affect the results as participants may agree with the person running the group even if that is not how they really feel.
[2 marks available — 1 mark for identifying a disadvantage and 1 mark for describing it]
The tendency for groups of people to agree with each other is sometimes called 'groupthink'. If people are interviewed individually, their opinions may be more likely to be their own.

9 (a) Any one from: e.g. Graphics should be related to food / There should be a navigation bar / There should be two text boxes and a button on the 'Rate a Restaurant' page / There should be a description of the AR feature and a box that displays the AR camera view. *[1 mark for correctly identifying one requirement]*

(b) E.g. The requirement about the app being accessible to a wide variety of users / The requirement that the font(s) and colour scheme used should make any text easy to read.
[1 mark for correctly identifying the requirement]
Fig. 2 tells you that one of the company's core values is inclusivity, so that is part of its ethos. You need to identify a requirement related to this value.

(c) E.g. a bell/'ding' sound / a trumpet sound *[1 mark]*
You'd get a mark for any reasonable suggestion here.

(d) Your wireframe layout may include the following:

Usual mobile app conventions
E.g. Navigation bars placed at the top or side of a page and positioned in the same place on all pages.
The shape of the app pages match conventional mobile phones, i.e. has a portrait layout.
In Fig. 3 the shape of the pages doesn't match this convention.

Useful labels
E.g. All boxes should have a label. For example, the box where the AR camera view will be displayed on the 'See Restaurants' page.
The labels should contain useful information. For example, instead of 'Description' as shown in Fig. 3 further detail could be given such as 'Description of the AR feature'.
You don't need to actually write a description of this feature on your wireframe, but it should be clear to anyone looking at it what the description there would be about.

Annotations showing the colours and how the pages link to each other
E.g. The colours should make the text clearly readable, as required by the client brief. So the text should be a colour that stands out on the background colour.
The layout should show how the pages link together, so there should be an annotation next to any buttons that move between pages to explain where they link to.

A layout that matches the client requirements and annotations to explain why the improved wireframe layout meets the requirements better
E.g. The layout should match the requirements for the 'Rate a Restaurant' page from the client brief. This was to contain two text boxes and a submit button.
The layout should have a navigation bar at the top of each page to go between the different pages.
How to grade your answer:

7-9 marks: The wireframe layout is comprehensive and shows detailed understanding. A range of suggested improvements are identified which cover a variety of components. Conventions are effectively applied. The answer clearly considers how suitable the layout is for the client's requirements.

4-6 marks: The wireframe layout is adequate and shows sound understanding. Some suggested improvements are identified which cover some components. Conventions are adequately applied. The answer makes some attempt to consider how suitable the wireframe layout is for the client's requirements.

1-3 marks: The wireframe layout is basic and shows limited understanding. Few suggested improvements are identified which cover few components. Conventions are applied in a limited way. The answer makes only a limited attempt to consider how suitable the wireframe layout is for the client's requirements.

0 marks: There is no relevant information.